TAKE CHARGE

((BE MONEY SMART))

IN

7

STEPS

CHRIS TEO
DR KOH N.K.

Marshall Cavendish
Editions

© 2022 Marshall Cavendish International (Asia) Private Limited
Text © Chris Teo & Dr Koh N.K.

Character design & illustrations by Chris Teo

Published by Marshall Cavendish Editions
An imprint of Marshall Cavendish International

A member of the
Times Publishing Group

Other Marshall Cavendish Offices:
Marshall Cavendish Corporation, 800 Westchester Ave, Suite N-641, Rye Brook, NY 10573,
USA • Marshall Cavendish International (Thailand) Co Ltd, 253 Asoke, 16th Floor, Sukhumvit
21 Road, Klongtoey Nua, Wattana, Bangkok 10110, Thailand • Marshall Cavendish (Malaysia)
Sdn Bhd, Times Subang, Lot 46, Subang Hi-Tech Industrial Park, Batu Tiga, 40000 Shah Alam,
Selangor Darul Ehsan, Malaysia

Marshall Cavendish is a registered trademark of Times Publishing Limited

National Library Board, Singapore Cataloguing-in-Publication Data

Name(s): Teo, Chris. | Koh, N. K., author.
Title: Take charge : be money smart in 7 steps / by Chris Teo, Dr Koh N K.
Description: Singapore : Marshall Cavendish Editions, 2022.
Identifier(s): ISBN 978-981-5009-77-4 (paperback)
Subject(s): LCSH: Young adults--Finance, Personal. | Financial literacy.
Classification: DDC 332.0240835--dc23

Printed in Singapore

CONTENTS

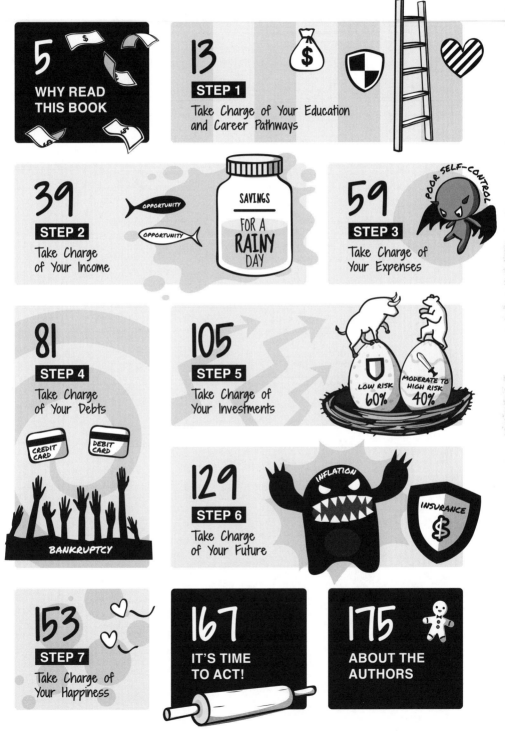

WHY READ THIS BOOK

Future-proof Your Financial Well-being with Gin & Friends

Once upon a time...

MORAL OF THE STORY

BE CAREFUL
WHO YOU TRUST.

MAKE INFORMED
DECISIONS TO TAKE
CHARGE OF YOUR MONEY.

WORK

Money is important

Money is a medium of exchange for goods and services that we need or want. We exchange our time, skills and efforts for money, and use that money to exchange for things such as books, food and movie tickets, or pay for services provided by other people, such as dental treatment or a haircut.

PAYDAY

EXCHANGE MONEY FOR NECESSITIES

7

We need necessities such as food, water and shelter to survive. In the past, people were self-sufficient; they grew their own vegetables, reared animals and drew water from the well. Today, we do not have to do any of these things. We can use the money we earn to exchange for necessities. What do you think will happen if we do not have money?

The money that you have is not infinite. You need to make smart financial decisions to manage your money, or you will be left with none.

People often make mistakes with their money at some point in their life. We will look at some common money mistakes to help you avoid painful financial pitfalls.

Money is a means, not an end in itself

Pop culture glamorises the rich and emphasises material purchases as an indicator of a happy life. People influenced by materialistic media messages believe that they need to be rich to be happy. They spend their life working towards this goal... but how rich is rich? And what happens after you become rich?

Some people spend their life working in a job which they do not like but continue to do so because it provides them with the means to live a lavish lifestyle. Happiness is sacrificed for money so that they can use the money to buy happiness, so they think... *does this even make sense to you?* It is a vicious cycle of working and spending because material possessions do not guarantee lasting happiness — most of the time, the happiness is temporary. Their search for happiness will never end.

We believe money is a means, not an end in itself. Money is not, and should not be, an end goal in life; it is just a means to get you to your goals. The promise of *Take Charge: Be Money Smart in 7 Steps* is this: you will learn to improve your financial well-being and develop your own life goals to long-lasting happiness. We will guide you step by step.

Save, Manage, Share

Here are three mantras to live by

We save whenever we can and make it a habit to save! Whether through grit or discipline, we must get into the habit of saving. If you haven't started saving regularly, start now — you will soon find saving like your second nature.

WHAT ARE MY GUIDING PRINCIPLES IN LIFE?

WHAT IS MY FINANCIAL GOAL?

WHAT MUST I DO TO ACHIEVE MY GOALS?

Managing your finances begins with envisioning your goals and principles in life. Financial planning is a process, not a product nor a destination. We will show you how.

Managing our finances well will mean we will have enough to share! As money is only a means, we amass it to be able to share with our loved ones and those who are less fortunate. It is a joy to be able to afford a comfortable lifestyle for our aged parents, or to have a nice meal with our friends to celebrate a birthday.

Come, we will journey with you!

STEP 1

Your destiny is in your hands!

We work to make money. A large portion of our adult life is spent working to buy necessities or the things that we want. The amount of time at work differs among companies, industries and countries. It is common in the US to work eight hours a day, five days a week. In China, some companies practise a 996-work culture where employees work from 9 am to 9 pm, six days per week!

We spend so much time at work that our job has a considerable impact on our happiness. "Do what you love, and you'll never work another day in your life" goes the old adage.

Striving for balance between happiness and money is one of the best things you can do for yourself as you venture out into the working world.

THE PATH TO MY DREAM JOB

LEAD DEVELOPER

SENIOR DEVELOPER

JUNIOR DEVELOPER

BACHELOR OF COMPUTING

DIPLOMA IN INFORMATION TECHNOLOGY

With so many different jobs in the global job market, it is possible to find one that interests you and pays well enough to cover your needs and wants for a comfortable lifestyle. But understand that most well-paying jobs require years of training and skills development. How do you plan to achieve your career goals?

THIS WAY

RIGHT PATH

GO HERE

Chart your career path

YOU NEED CERTIFICATION TO GET THAT JOB

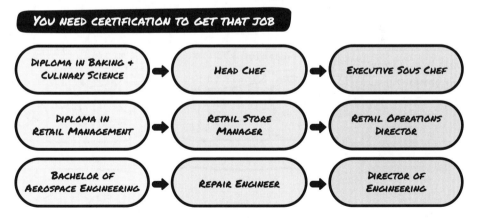

Diploma in Baking + Culinary Science	➡	Head Chef	➡	Executive Sous Chef
Diploma in Retail Management	➡	Retail Store Manager	➡	Retail Operations Director
Bachelor of Aerospace Engineering	➡	Repair Engineer	➡	Director of Engineering

Choosing a career pathway is a serious matter as what you do will have profound effects on your life. Avoid negative mindsets such as "I don't know what I want to do". Make ***informed decisions*** to manage your career pathway. A wrong career choice will make you miserable and you will need time to get back on the right track.

Keep in mind the following guiding principles as you start thinking about your career.

Do not **blindly embark** on a certain career path because someone tells you to do so.

Do not **follow your peers** without thinking about what is best for you.

Do not select a path that is most **convenient** to you.

Do not be **biased**. Keep an open mind.

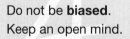

ACCOUNTING

BUSINESS

ARTS

HEALTHCARE

As the saying goes, a frog in the well can only see a small circle of the sky. So, first things first, widen your horizon and discover new career possibilities. Find out about the different industries and how they contribute to society (Google is your best friend).

Here is a simple exercise to get you thinking. In the worksheet on the next page, list **10 industries** that appeal to you.

AVIATION

MANUFACTURING

FOOD AND BEVERAGE

WORKSHEET 1

Ten industries that I find appealing

Here are more examples: Accounting and Legal, Arts, Aviation, Business, Construction, Civil Service, Education, Finance, Food and Beverage, Healthcare, Hospitality, Information Technology, Logistics, Manufacturing, Media, Real Estate, Retail, Tourism, Oil and Gas

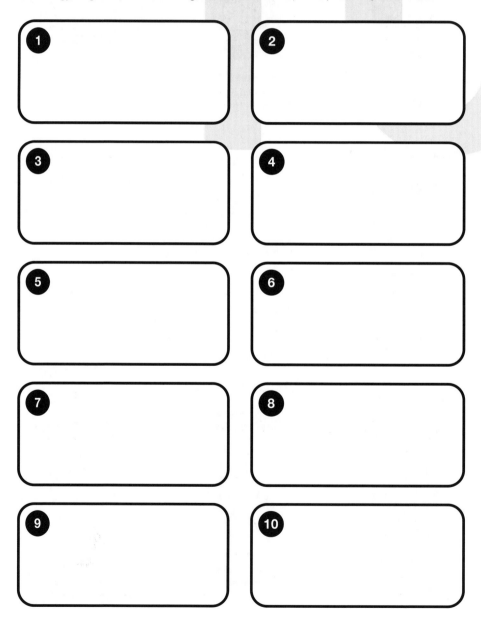

Next, discover the different job opportunities within the 10 industries you have listed.

For each job you have identified, find out more about it — job function, working hours, work environment, job progression and average salary.

JOB OPPORTUNITIES IN THE MEDIA INDUSTRY

Art Director Brand Strategist
Sub Editor Content Manager
Photographer **Interpreter**
Digital Marketing Manager
Blogger Journalist
Online Community Manager
Writer Video Editor
Public Relations Specialist
Graphic Designer **Actor** Camera Operator
Marketing Manager Choreographer
Communications Director Sound technician

JOB RESEARCH

SOLDIER
Defend and protect our country from external attacks

Working Hours
Irregular

Work Environment
Army camp

Average Salary
💰💰💰

Job Progression
RECRUIT ➡ SOLDIER ➡ COMMANDER

ACCOUNTANT
Record monetary transactions and prepare tax returns

Working Hours
Normal office hours

Work Environment
Office

Average Salary
💰💰💰💰

Job Progression
ACCOUNTANT ➡ CONTROLLER ➡ CFO

Now list **20 jobs** that you find appealing in the worksheet on the next page.

WORKSHEET 2

Twenty jobs that I find appealing

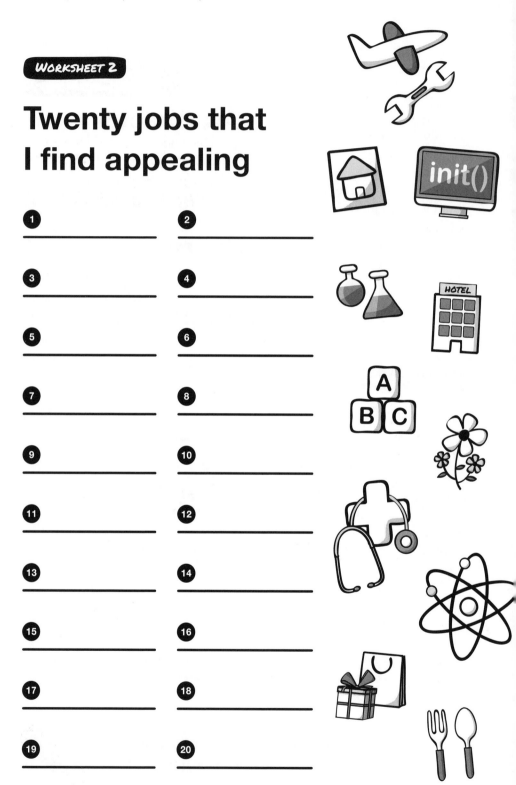

1 _____

2 _____

3 _____

4 _____

5 _____

6 _____

7 _____

8 _____

9 _____

10 _____

11 _____

12 _____

13 _____

14 _____

15 _____

16 _____

17 _____

18 _____

19 _____

20 _____

Money, Mind and Heart

Well done! You have expanded your career options. Let's now filter your choices using three criteria: Money, Mind and Heart.

DO I HAVE ENOUGH MONEY FOR MY LIVING EXPENSES?

1. SALARY AND CAREER PROGRESSION (MONEY)

When you leave school and start to work, you will no longer receive an allowance from your parents. You will have to start paying for your own mobile phone bill, transport and meals, and perhaps even contributing to your family's household expenses. You may also have a study loan to repay or want to buy insurance. Think about your financial commitments, expenses and aspirations.

WORKSHEET 3

What is the estimated minimum amount of money you need for your monthly financial commitments and expenses?

$ _____

Scan here to view national average household expenses.

What is the amount of money you hope to make every month?

$ _____

Scan here to view median monthly salary.

Now go back to Worksheet 2 and strike off the jobs that pay less than your estimated expenses. You need to consider jobs that pay enough to cover your expenses.

Career progression is the process of advancing and being promoted in your job — working up the ranks. Promotion leads to a better title and higher pay.

Different jobs and industries have different career progressions. Good companies make employee development a priority and help move employees up the career ladder.

Note that you should not select jobs based solely on starting pay. Consider also the career progression opportunities and income potential. With the right attitude and skill sets, a junior executive with a low starting pay can work their way up to management.

Job security is the assurance that you are not in danger of losing your job. For context, we refer to job security as security with your job skills within an industry.

During the COVID-19 pandemic, many jobs were made redundant due to the lack of economic activity. Workers were retrenched and many were unable to find a new job. Those with little savings fared the worst as they were now left without a salary. We will share how you can protect yourself from financial crises in Step 6.

Not all jobs are created equal. While most industries shrank during the pandemic, the healthcare and information technology industries expanded. In healthcare, the pandemic drove up staffing needs for new roles to manage COVID-19 patients and support testing operations.

23

The pandemic also sped up the adoption of digital technology when people had to work from home. Even teachers and students were affected as classes went online. All these led to rising demand for IT experts.

With technology and automation on the rise, some jobs may not exist for long. Self-service terminals might replace cashiers, and self-driving cars might replace private hire drivers.

Try to identify future demands in the job market and research carefully. Don't waste your time on a 'soon-to-be-obsolete' career.

3. PASSION (HEART)

Passion for work is the enthusiasm and excitement we have for the work we do. Work is enjoyable and we are more productive in our job. Passion creates a drive that motivates us to pursue excellence instead of doing something for the sake of doing it. We care deeply about what we do and are personally invested in our job.

People who are passionate about their work tend to be happier and have a higher potential for achieving career success. There are three main factors that drive passion for work: interest, environment and purpose.

I WANT TO BE THE VERY BEST I CAN BE.

STEP 1

Interest

Career interest is your preferences for specific work activities. You can take the Holland Codes Test to identify where your interests lie and discover jobs that correspond with those interests.

The Holland Codes is a theory of careers choice developed by American psychologist John Holland. The six main career interest areas are Conventional, Investigative, Social, Artistic, Realistic and Enterprising. For example, people in the Artistic interest group prefer jobs that allow expressive freedom, while people in the Enterprising interest group prefer a leadership role.

CONVENTIONAL   INVESTIGATIVE

SOCIAL   ARTISTIC

REALISTIC   ENTERPRISING

Scan here for Holland Codes Test.

TAKE NOTE!

The Holland Codes is a helpful tool to learn more about your interests and what they mean for you based on your personality. Keep an open mind, and do not restrict yourself to the results. After all, your destiny is in your hands!

Environment

The work environment is the surroundings or conditions in which people work. It encompasses the physical settings and the psychosocial environment.

I LOVE MY WORKPLACE.

Physical settings refer to the physical location — such as the office, school, shopping mall, amusement park, stadium or zoo. It also includes workplace equipment such as machinery if you are an engineer or ultrasound machines if you are a medical technician.

Psychosocial environment refers to the interpersonal and social interactions in the workplace between colleagues or customers. Some people prefer to work alone while others prefer to collaborate and work in teams.

Consider your personality type when choosing the psychosocial environment. An introvert who does not function well in a team can be misunderstood as unfriendly and lazy. An extrovert working alone might feel despondent from the lack of interaction.

Purpose

Why do we do the work we do? Every job exists for a reason!

TEACHERS EDUCATE AND PREPARE THEIR STUDENTS FOR THE CHALLENGES OF TOMORROW.

CLEANERS KEEP THE ENVIRONMENT CLEAN AND TIDY.

FARMERS GROW FOOD TO FEED THE HUNGRY WORLD.

DOCTORS SAVE LIVES AND WATCH OVER PEOPLE'S HEALTH.

I STEP UP, I CONTRIBUTE, I MAKE A DIFFERENCE!

Those who feel their work contributes to a larger cause are much more likely to find their jobs fulfilling. Even trivial tasks feel significant! They take great pride in their job, knowing how their efforts make the world a better place for someone else.

Having a passion for work will keep you engaged and satisfied. Go on a journey of self-discovery and determine how you feel about the jobs you listed in Worksheet 2 in relation to your interests, the environment and purpose. For now, don't worry if you do not have suitable skill sets. Instead, focus on the enjoyment you think you will derive from the job and not what you are good at.

DEFINE YOUR PURPOSE

I BAKE CAKES.

I MAKE CUSTOMERS HAPPY WITH MY SWEET TREATS.

Your passion for work can change as you grow older or progress professionally. You might discover careers that you are more passionate about or uncover new purposes in life. Technology may open new career pathways that were not available in the past. Your priorities may change, with marriage and a family of your own. There are many other factors to consider in choosing a job. When you do a reality check, you may find that you cannot choose a job based just on your passion.

IN A NUTSHELL

Different career paths have different **income potential**.

Different career paths create different levels of **job satisfaction**.

Different career paths provide different levels of **job security**.

WORKSHEET 4

Finding the right balance

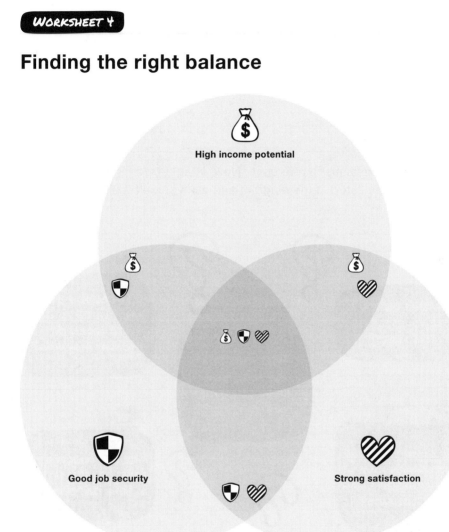

Instructions

1) Go through the jobs listed in Worksheet 2 (page 20) and **write** them into their respective sections in the Venn diagram above.

2) Money is important. Now **circle** those jobs that can potentially pay more than your ideal salary as listed in Worksheet 3 (page 21).

3) Job security gives you peace of mind. **Underline** three jobs that offer the most security, based on your research.

4) You cannot live on passion alone, but it will be miserable to work without passion. **Draw** a heart beside your top three favourite jobs.

Look at your responses in the Venn diagram. Jobs in the middle of the diagram have high earning potential, good job security, and might give you a strong sense of satisfaction. However, do not restrict yourself to those jobs.

The Venn diagram is just a reference. Now, imagine working in one of the jobs that you listed in the diagram and ask yourself the following five questions.

WHERE DO YOU SEE YOURSELF IN FIVE YEARS?

WILL THIS JOB SUPPORT YOUR IDEAL LIFESTYLE IN FIVE YEARS?

WILL YOU BE MOTIVATED TO GO TO WORK ON MONDAY MORNING?

WILL YOU BE PROUD TO SHARE YOUR WORK ACTIVITIES WITH FRIENDS?

ARE YOU WILLING TO DEVELOP NEW SKILLS FOR THIS JOB?

The three criteria — Money, Mind and Heart — and the five questions will help you find the right career path. Choosing a career path is a life-changing decision. You need to take full responsibility for your choices and accept the consequences of your actions. Weigh all options before you make your decision!

WORKSHEET 5

Name your ideal job

Embark on your path

Charting a career pathway is just the start of your journey. Let's now plot mini steps to move forward. Fill in the worksheet below.

Hint: You can find out the job requirements from job postings on recruitment websites.

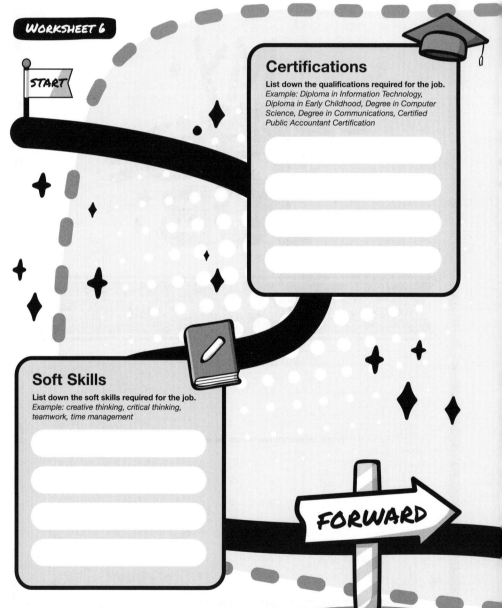

WORKSHEET 6

START

Certifications

List down the qualifications required for the job.
Example: Diploma in Information Technology, Diploma in Early Childhood, Degree in Computer Science, Degree in Communications, Certified Public Accountant Certification

Soft Skills

List down the soft skills required for the job.
Example: creative thinking, critical thinking, teamwork, time management

FORWARD

STEP 1

Job Progression

List down the job progression milestones.
Example:
Junior Designer > Designer > Art Director

Computer Skills

List down the computer skills required for the job.
Example: Adobe Photoshop, Final Cut Pro, Microsoft Office, Google Suite

Worksheet 6, which you have just completed, is a useful exercise to help you get started on charting your career path.

But a plan is nothing without action. Get up and make it happen! Start by researching schools that offer relevant courses and certifications. But note that not all schools are equal — some companies might have hiring preferences over certain schools, even though the certificate is the same.

Paper qualifications alone are not enough to win out the job competition — you need to stand out among your competitors. Find out what other technical skills are required for the job and plan to acquire them. Employers also value soft skills, such as communicating well with colleagues, teamwork, problem solving and others, so develop these skills too. There are lots of free online resources that you can tap on or you can explore online courses from reputed institutes. The schedule is usually flexible and you learn at your own pace.

WORKSHEET 7

Online resources

Explore the Internet for courses that interest you and that will help you develop new skills. List them below.

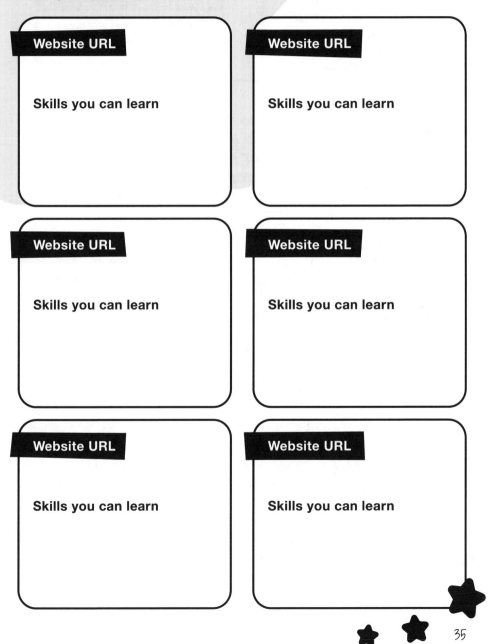

Website URL

Skills you can learn

Website URL

Skills you can learn

Website URL

Skills you can learn

Website URL

Skills you can learn

Website URL

Skills you can learn

Website URL

Skills you can learn

You can also join online communities and network with people with similar interests or in the same work industry. You will get advice from mentors and even inside information on job opportunities.

By taking charge of your education and career pathways, you will have a clear picture of your career goals and the steps required to reach your destination. You can focus on moving forward without sidetracking. However, life doesn't always go according to plan and you have to be prepared for obstacles and roadblocks in your path. You need to have a positive mindset to overcome challenges.

Follow through with your plans as much as possible but be flexible enough to change if dire situations arise. For example, the tourism and aviation industries were badly hit by the COVID-19 pandemic and many people lost their jobs. Recovery is slow and uncertain. When faced with such a situation, you will need to make a decision — do you keep to your career path or do you embark on a new path?

TL;DR

1 There are different types of job opportunities in the market.

2 Narrow down your career options based on salary, career progression, job security and passion.

3 Get the relevant qualifications and skills for the career you have chosen.

What is income?

Income means money received on a regular basis. There are two categories of income: active income and passive income. Active income is money earned in exchange for your labour and effort. Passive income is money that requires little to no effort to earn and is usually obtained through investments.

EFFORT REQUIRED

ACTIVE INCOME

LITTLE TO NO EFFORT

PASSIVE INCOME

The primary source of income for most people is from active income. You receive money for the work you do, either from your employer or from running your own business.

Your income will change over your lifetime; factors such as career progression, the state of the economy and the financial decisions you make will have a significant impact on your income potential.

DO YOU KNOW?
When you are employed, you enjoy benefits such as paid leave and health insurance.

EMPLOYED VS SELF-EMPLOYED

Being employed provides stability and predictability. Knowing how much salary you receive at the end of each month allows you to make better financial decisions. However, your income potential is capped largely based on your salary.

You need to work hard even if your salary is capped!

Being self-employed provides you with the flexibility to choose your working hours or the type of work you do. Your income potential is higher as it is possible to scale your operation or hire more people to expand your business. However, your income can be irregular, and you can even make a loss! Being your own boss may not be a suitable option, especially if you have heavy financial commitments. You sacrifice security for freedom.

STEP 2

THE BEST OF BOTH WORLDS?

As you can see, there are pros and cons to being employed by a company or being your own boss.

There is a third option: you can run a side business or take on freelance work to supplement your primary income. A second job can even be seen as a safety net in case you lose your day job.

The downside to having a second job is a poor work-life balance. You will be spending much more time at work at the expense of rest and leisure. Not having enough rest might lead to poor work performance and burnout. You are possibly sacrificing your health for money. You need to strike the right balance to preserve your health!

Some companies have policies or employment clauses that restrict a second job. Even if there are no restrictions, your immediate supervisor and co-workers might frown upon your second job if it affects your performance.

THE GIG ECONOMY

The rise of on-demand digital platforms, such as Grab and Food Panda, has led to an increased demand for low-skilled gig workers. A gig worker is a person who has a temporary job, usually in the service sector, or has a formal agreement with companies to provide ad hoc services on their platform. The company usually takes a cut from the gig worker's earnings on top of their platform's service fee.

STEP 2

Typical gig jobs include private hire driver and food delivery. Such jobs are mostly taken up by people needing additional income on top of their day job or as a stopgap solution before finding full-time employment.

43

Some people prefer gig work because of the flexible working hours which allow them to pursue other interests. Gig jobs, however, do not offer employment benefits such as paid leave, health insurance or protection from unfair dismissal. There is also no career progression. It is not advisable to do gig work permanently as the income potential is low and platform owners can change the contractual terms or commission rate anytime.

Three ways to increase income

The amount of money you make during your lifetime is dependent on your life choices. Do you want to make more money? I do! We all want to earn more money, but not everyone has the know-how or motivation to act. Here are some ways to increase income.

STEP 2

LEVEL UP

YOU ARE PROMOTED TO MANAGER!

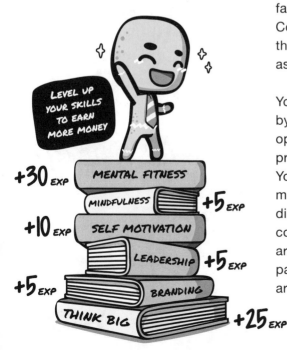

LEVEL UP YOUR SKILLS TO EARN MORE MONEY

+30 EXP — MENTAL FITNESS
MINDFULNESS +5 EXP
+10 EXP — SELF MOTIVATION
LEADERSHIP +5 EXP
+5 EXP — BRANDING
THINK BIG +25 EXP

1. Grow your career

The most common way to make more money is to grow your salary, and the way to grow your salary faster is to get promoted. Companies promote staff whom they value because they are an asset to the business.

You can get better at what you do by taking up on-the-job training opportunities or attending relevant professional development courses. You can also volunteer to take on more responsibilities that will directly contribute to your company's success. Companies are more likely to chart a career path for employees who they see are contributing more.

45

2. TAKE ON A FREELANCE JOB

What if promotion opportunities are limited due to workplace competition or economic conditions? You can consider taking on freelance projects to supplement your income. A freelancer is a person who offers services and earns money on a per-project basis.

EXAMPLES OF FREELANCE JOBS

You can develop a diverse skill set by signing up for different professional development courses. Having a new skill will open up more freelance job opportunities. Freelance projects that require in-demand skills can be lucrative.

Visit jobs websites such as fiverr.com or upwork.com to find out what the market is looking for and the remuneration.

BEING A JACK-OF-ALL-TRADES GIVES YOU MORE FREELANCE OPPORTUNITIES.

Scan here for freelancing platforms.

3. INVEST YOUR MONEY

We invest money to grow our income and build up our savings to prepare for retirement. You can buy stocks and bonds or property to grow your income through dividends or capital appreciation. This is passive income, and we'll discuss this in Step 5. Instead of working for money, make money work for you!

EARNED INCOME:
EXCHANGE LABOUR FOR MONEY

SALARY
$1,000

INVESTMENT INCOME:
EXCHANGE MONEY FOR MORE MONEY

DIVIDENDS
$500

STEP 2

You need a budget to manage your income

A budget is a plan to allocate your income. A good budget will help increase your potential income and prepare you for the major life milestones such as marriage, buying a home, raising a family and retirement.

BUDGETING IS A LIFELONG FINANCIAL HABIT

I SPEND CAUTIOUSLY AND SHARE THE FRUITS OF MY LABOUR WITH MY LOVED ONES.

I SPEND WISELY AND INVEST TO GROW MY INCOME POTENTIAL.

I SPEND RESPONSIBLY AND SAVE AS MUCH AS I CAN.

POCKET MONEY

SALARY

RETIREMENT FUNDS

47

You need to make **informed decisions** to create a budget and discipline yourself to follow the plan. Here is a modified version of the "6 Money Jars System" popularised by T. Harv Eker to help you create your budget.

Money Jar #1: Daily Expenses

The money in this jar is for daily expenses, such as transport and meals, or anything you consider to be a necessity. Be honest about what you need! You should always think before you spend but you do not need to be overly frugal. Any adjustments to this jar will have an immediate impact on your standard of living.

THE BEST INVESTMENT YOU CAN MAKE IS IN YOURSELF.

WARREN BUFFETT

Money Jar #2: Self-Improvement

The money in this jar is for personal and professional skills development through courses and certifications. Automation and digitalisation continuously drive changes in the world of work. You should constantly upgrade your work skills to stay relevant and increase your income potential.

LEARN MORE, EARN MORE.

Money Jar #3: Play

All work and no play makes Jack a dull boy. You can allocate a small amount of money every month to treat yourself to a movie, dinner at a nice restaurant or anything you want. Having a spending cap on the 'play' expenses is helpful, especially if you tend to overspend. Be aware that every cent allocated into the play jar means less money for investments.

Money Jar #4: Share

Money in this jar is for sharing with your loved ones, donating to worthy causes or helping the less fortunate. Buy a gift to surprise your family or treat your friends to dinner. You can also donate money and necessities to charity. Helping others will give you a sense of purpose and satisfaction in life. Giving is a joy and it is a blessing to give than to receive.

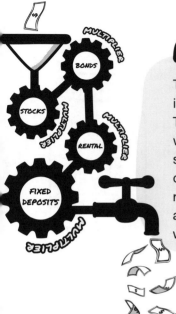

MONEY JAR #5: INVESTMENT

The money in this jar is for you to invest and to grow your money. There are many ways to invest and we cover this in Step 5. Investing small amounts of money steadily over time can generate significant returns. The more money you allocate into this jar, the more you will have in future.

PUT YOUR MONEY ON AUTOPILOT TO MAKE MORE MONEY

MONEY JAR #6: SAVINGS

We save money so that we will have enough to spend in the future. By putting money into this jar, you will grow your savings and build a financial safety net. You can use part of your savings for major expenses when the need arises. We split savings into two parts: emergency fund and non-emergency fund.

EMERGENCY FUND

NON-EMERGENCY FUND

Emergency fund

An emergency fund is necessary to tide you over when difficult times arise. A sudden loss of income can happen to anyone, including you. You might fall sick and cannot work; or you might lose your job because your company is downsizing or closing for good. Without an income, you won't have money to pay for necessities or fulfil your financial commitments. You might even fall into debt! In such times you will have to depend on your savings.

Creating an emergency fund should be your top financial priority as it is meant to cover your expenses while you search for a new job. Ideally, you should have enough money for at least six months' worth of expenses and financial commitments. This amount can be substantial, so start saving as soon as possible.

51

Non-emergency fund

You use your non-emergency fund to purchase big-ticket items, such as a holiday or the latest gaming computer.

For some people, however, saving up for expensive things can seem unachievable and they choose to buy on credit to receive the item immediately. But do you know that you will pay more when you buy on credit?

I CAN PAY $50,000 AT ONCE OR PAY $55,000 OVER 10 MONTHS.

SALE $50,000

BIG-TICKET ITEMS SEEM MORE AFFORDABLE WHEN YOU PAY IN MONTHLY INSTALMENTS

1 $5,500 2 $5,500 3 $5,500 4 $5,500 5 $5,500 6 $5,500 7 $5,500 8 $5,500 9 $5,500 10 $5,500

Avoid the temptation of resorting to easy credit for non-essential items; if you must buy something you do not really need, pay with cash that you have saved up. If you have no savings, then hold off the purchase. Practise delayed gratification (more on this in Step 3) and take small but regular steps to grow your non-emergency fund.

Budgeting and financial well-being

Let's look at the profiles of the characters you have met to see how budgeting affects their financial well-being.

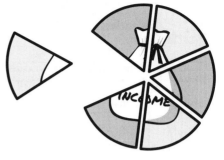

HORSE
MRS FRUGAL

INCOME POTENTIAL

FINANCIAL SECURITY
☆ ☆ ☆ ☆

DAILY EXPENSES	SELF IMPROVEMENT	PLAY	SHARE	INVESTMENT	SAVINGS
20%	0%	0%	0%	0%	80%

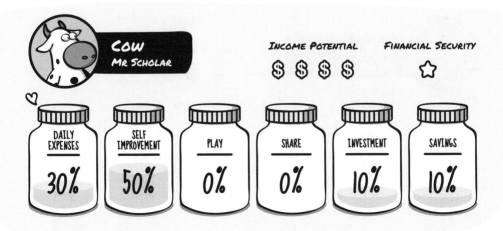

COW
MR SCHOLAR

INCOME POTENTIAL
$ $ $

FINANCIAL SECURITY
☆

DAILY EXPENSES	SELF IMPROVEMENT	PLAY	SHARE	INVESTMENT	SAVINGS
30%	50%	0%	0%	10%	10%

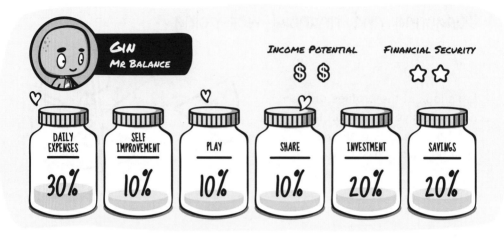

GIN
MR BALANCE

INCOME POTENTIAL
$ $

FINANCIAL SECURITY
☆ ☆

DAILY EXPENSES	SELF IMPROVEMENT	PLAY	SHARE	INVESTMENT	SAVINGS
30%	10%	10%	10%	20%	20%

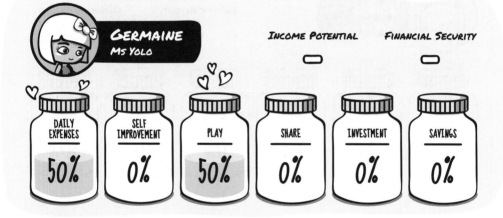

GERMAINE
MS YOLO

INCOME POTENTIAL
▭

FINANCIAL SECURITY
▭

DAILY EXPENSES	SELF IMPROVEMENT	PLAY	SHARE	INVESTMENT	SAVINGS
50%	0%	50%	0%	0%	0%

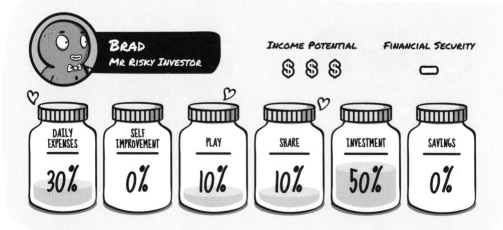

BRAD
MR RISKY INVESTOR

INCOME POTENTIAL
$ $ $

FINANCIAL SECURITY
▭

DAILY EXPENSES	SELF IMPROVEMENT	PLAY	SHARE	INVESTMENT	SAVINGS
30%	0%	10%	10%	50%	0%

Three rules to help you plan your budget

Allocating your money prudently will help you increase your income potential and prepare you for unexpected emergencies. However, creating a budget is just the beginning of a long journey. You need to be disciplined and stick to your budget.

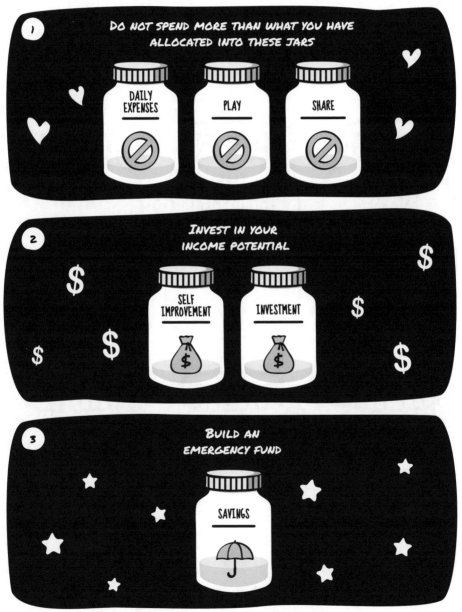

1 DO NOT SPEND MORE THAN WHAT YOU HAVE ALLOCATED INTO THESE JARS

DAILY EXPENSES | PLAY | SHARE

2 INVEST IN YOUR INCOME POTENTIAL

SELF IMPROVEMENT | INVESTMENT

3 BUILD AN EMERGENCY FUND

SAVINGS

WORKSHEET 8

Create your own budget

My income after deducting financial commitments

DAILY EXPENSES

SELF IMPROVEMENT

PLAY

SHARE

INVESTMENT

SAVINGS

Sticking to the budget you have set for yourself will stop you from overspending and help you reach your financial goals. You will feel more confident, knowing that you are in control of your finances. If you fail to plan, you are planning to fail.

TL;DR

1. Create a budget to allocate your income efficiently and avoid overspending.

2. Divide your income into these six categories: daily expenses, self-improvement, play, share, investment and savings.

3. Manage your income well so that you have plenty to share.

4. Build an emergency fund to cover your expenses in times of need.

5. Grow your active and passive income to earn more money.

STEP 3

What is expense?

Expense is money that is spent to buy something, such as food, clothes, utilities, entertainment or education. You need to make **informed decisions** and prioritise spending on what is essential and cut back spending on the non-essential items.

I HAVE $500. SHOULD I BUY NEW CLOTHES OR A NEW LAPTOP?

NEEDS AND WANTS

You need food, water and shelter. You need clothes to wear and computers to learn. 'Needs' are the essential things for you to live in society. 'Wants' are non-essential things that you desire and are good or nice to have, but you can live without.

How do you decide if something is a need or a want? It depends on your perspective and circumstances. Food is a need, but the expensive food served at a fancy restaurant is a want. A computer is a need if you use it for learning or work. The same computer becomes a want if you only use it to watch movies on Netflix.

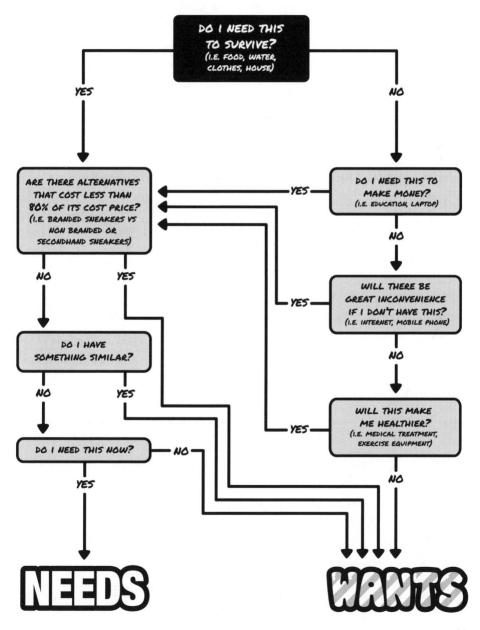

STEP 3

BEING MINDFUL OF YOUR SPENDING DOESN'T MEAN YOU HAVE TO SKIP YOUR DAILY ENERGY BOOSTER. LOOK OUT FOR ALTERNATIVES THAT COST LESS.

Instant gratification vs delayed gratification

In Step 2, you learnt to create a budget to avoid overspending. With the limited amount of money allocated for expenses, you should prioritise spending on your needs over your wants. Some people cannot control their impulses and succumb to instant gratification — when they want something, they want it immediately. Those who lack self-control tend to overspend and get into financial difficulties. Have you bought something on impulse, and it is still unused in your wardrobe?

The opposite of instant gratification is delayed gratification. This is the ability to resist the temptation of wanting an immediate reward in anticipation of a greater reward later. Temptations often pop up and create desires that distract you from your goals. Learn to delay gratification and get into the habit of delaying gratification — it will help you focus better and achieve your life goals faster.

STEP 3

Financial commitments

A financial commitment is a commitment to an expense at a future date. There will be a penalty if you cannot pay and fulfil your commitment on time. You can even be made bankrupt in the worst-case scenario!

TYPE	PENALTY
⚡ UTILITY BILLS	Power and water disruption
🏠 RENT	Termination of lease and forfeit of deposit
🛡 INSURANCE PAYMENT	Loss of coverage
💳 CREDIT CARD PAYMENT	Higher interest rates and damage to your credit score
📄 LOAN REPAYMENT	Lawsuit

Always ask yourself if you can afford the item before committing to it. Once you sign the contract, you must prioritise to fulfil the commitment in a timely manner.

Live within your means

To live within your means is to spend less than your income. You are living within your means when you have enough money for all your expenses and do not need to take loans and be in debt.

These days it can be challenging to resist the urge to spend when we are bombarded with tempting advertisements every day.

We also tend to overspend when we have easy access to credit. Credit cards and short-term loan schemes like Buy Now Pay Later (BNPL) are catalysts that entice us to spend more than our income allows us to. It is very easy for those who cannot resist the temptation to spend to end up in debt.

65

Four ways to help you control spending

1 When you feel tempted to buy an item you don't really need, distract yourself with other activities. Read a book or go for a walk.

2 Practise delayed gratification.

3 Overcome the spending urge by focusing on your long-term financial and life goals.

4 Do not take a loan for want items. If you must spend, use cash or a debit card where money is directly deducted from your bank account to make the payment.

Four ways to get the most out of your money

In Step 2, you learnt to allocate a sum of money towards expenses. Now get the most out of your money with these four simple tips: compare prices, take advantage of sales, buy preloved items, and opt for no-spend or affordable activities.

1. COMPARE PRICES

As creatures of habit, we tend to do our shopping at the same store. If there is an item you need to buy, say a laptop, find out what other stores are charging for the same laptop first. Online retailers often have special deals as well. You will notice that prices can vary for the same item. The price difference can be huge for big-ticket items.

STEP 3

2. TAKE ADVANTAGE OF SALES

Look out for annual sales or special sales events tied to specific products. At such times, the price of goods is marked down and good deals are offered. Stores often run such promotions to attract sales and clear stock. Keep a look out for such events on the store's website or social media pages, or join relevant social media groups to keep yourself up to date.

> **TAKE NOTE!**
> Be wary of unethical and gimmicky sales promotions. These can mislead you into believing you are getting a good deal.

3. BUY PRELOVED ITEMS

Preloved is a term used to describe something pre-owned or secondhand, and includes items such as jewellery, books, toys, sports equipment and furniture. These can be just as good as new items especially if they are well maintained. Furthermore, they cost less. It is possible to enjoy reduced prices without compromising on quality.

Buying preloved is also better for the environment because you are recycling and reusing the item. New products require raw materials to manufacture, depleting the earth's resources. When you purchase a preloved product, you prevent waste from reaching landfills. You are a protector of Mother Earth!

Online classifieds and listing platforms have driven a surge in secondhand shopping. You can easily download an app to buy or sell preloved items. The next time you want to buy something, search for it first on a secondhand listing platform. You will save money and the environment at the same time!

Scan here for online classifieds and listing platforms.

TAKE NOTE!

Buying preloved might be smart on your wallet and a benefit to the planet, but it also comes with hidden costs and some risks.

Repair costs

Secondhand items such as electronics and cars may need repair works due to faulty parts or wear-and-tear. You should check carefully for defects and consider the cost of potential repairs before purchasing such items.

Safety

Some secondhand products might look fine on the outside but have structural problems that can be dangerous. Avoid buying safety equipment such as helmets or car brakes if you cannot inspect the item physically. Your well-being is more important than the money saved.

When buying preloved furniture, ensure that the legs and base of the item are not cracked. The furniture should not have missing parts and must be stable. You do not want to injure yourself and pay for expensive medical treatment.

Personal hygiene

Preloved items such as clothes and jewellery may still have traces of the previous owner's sweat and germs. In extreme cases, you can get skin rashes and serious infections. Check for stains and weird smells before buying. When you have bought the item, wash and clean it before use.

Do not be discouraged by the risks associated with preloved products and miss out on a good deal. Be a savvy shopper and know what to look out for when purchasing such items. Be vigilant and cautious!

4. OPT FOR NO-SPEND AND AFFORDABLE ACTIVITIES

Are you one of those who can't wait for Friday to come (TGIF!)? Many of us count the days and hours to the weekend. When the rest day finally comes, we just want to go out and spend money to unwind. While a trip to the spa or a quick massage can recharge you for the new work week ahead, these activities will eat into your budget.

You want to rewind, relax and have fun on your rest days. At the same time, you need to cut back on spending to achieve your financial and life goals. Fortunately, there are many free and affordable activities you can do during your rest days.

OUTDOOR IDEAS

FREE

Check out the exhibits
at a public museum.

Just don't break anything.

OUTDOOR IDEAS

FREE

Take a walk in the park or
explore a nature reserve.

Bring your own water bottle.

OUTDOOR IDEAS

AFFORDABLE

Fish a fish.

*You need to own fishing equipment
and buy lures for each trip.*

OUTDOOR IDEAS

AFFORDABLE

FREE

Go for a cycle.

*Free if you already own a bike.
Affordable if you rent one for a
few hours.*

OUTDOOR IDEAS

FREE

Volunteer at a pet shelter.

Bring some pet treats if you want.

OUTDOOR IDEAS

FREE

Relax on the beach.

Bring suntan lotion.

INDOOR IDEAS

FREE

Do yoga or meditate.

*Free if you follow along on YouTube.
Wear something comfortable.*

INDOOR IDEAS

MEOW AFFORDABLE

Hang out with friends at home.

Binge-watch to unwind and de-stress.

INDOOR IDEAS

AFFORDABLE

Grow your own indoor edibles.

Yummy!

INDOOR IDEAS

AFFORDABLE

Cook up a feast.

Cooking is cheaper than eating out.

INDOOR IDEAS

AFFORDABLE

FREE

Read a book.

*Affordable. A good book is worth
every penny. Free if you borrow
from the library.*

INDOOR IDEAS

FREE

Clean and declutter
your house.

*A clean house makes you
happier and less stressed.*

STEP 3

WORKSHEET 9

Come up with your own ideas to unwind and jot them down below. When you're bored, scan the QR code and do the activity corresponding to the number displayed.

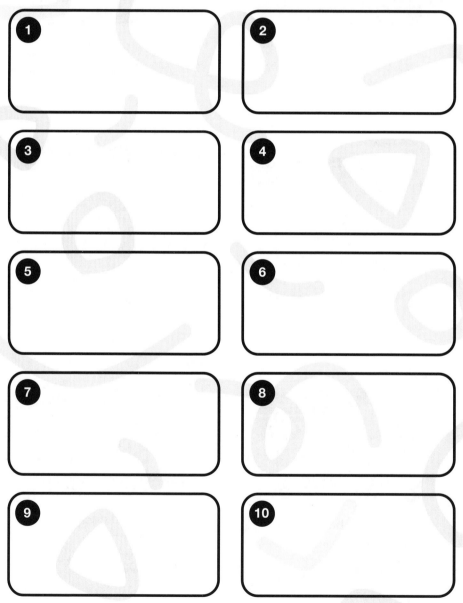

Penny wise, pound foolish

MOVIES

TRANSPORT

This chapter is about cutting expenses. People who get into the habit of cutting expenses may want to reduce costs in **all** aspects of their life. But there are times when you should **not** cut your expenses. There are things in life that you cannot afford to skimp on. Be careful not to be penny wise, pound foolish.

PREVENTIVE HEALTHCARE

FINE DINING

HOUSEHOLD REPAIRS

OVERSEAS TRIPS

STEP 3

PREVENTIVE HEALTHCARE

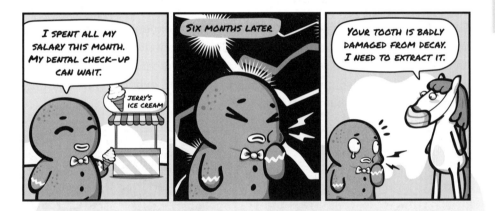

> I SPENT ALL MY SALARY THIS MONTH. MY DENTAL CHECK-UP CAN WAIT.

JERRY'S ICE CREAM

SIX MONTHS LATER

> YOUR TOOTH IS BADLY DAMAGED FROM DECAY. I NEED TO EXTRACT IT.

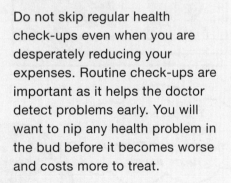

> REMOVING MY TOOTH COST MUCH MORE THAN A REGULAR DENTAL CHECK-UP!

Do not skip regular health check-ups even when you are desperately reducing your expenses. Routine check-ups are important as it helps the doctor detect problems early. You will want to nip any health problem in the bud before it becomes worse and costs more to treat.

77

Healthcare is costly and can make a big dent in your savings! However, spending money on your personal well-being and living a healthy lifestyle is the surest way to reduce massive healthcare expenses in the future.

AN APPLE A DAY KEEPS MEDICAL BILLS AWAY

MEDICAL BILL $100

$1

REGULAR UPKEEP AND REPAIRS

Buying a car or a house is not just a one-time expense — you need to spend money to keep them in good condition. A poorly maintained vehicle can be a safety hazard. A faulty power socket can cause fire and damage your electrical appliances. Do not skimp on these expenses, or you may wind up with a hefty bill in the long run.

THERE ARE WEIRD NOISES COMING OUT FROM THE OVEN... I WILL FIX IT WHEN I FEEL RICH.

BUZZ

MY KITCHEN IS RUINED!

BOOM

I SHOULD HAVE REPAIRED MY OVEN THE MOMENT I HEARD THOSE NOISES.

BYE BYE

NEW FRIDGE

MEDICAL BILL

KITCHEN REPAIR WORKS

NEW OVEN

These are some of the major expenses you
will incur when you own a car or house.

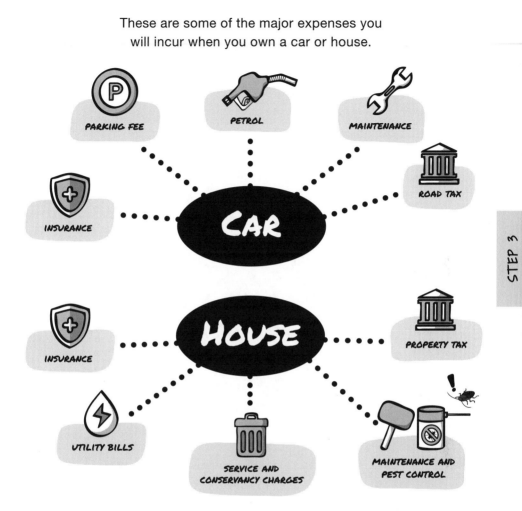

TL;DR

1. Prioritise your needs and wants.

2. Resist the temptation to buy and control your spending habits.

3. Make every dollar count but do not be penny wise, pound foolish.

STEP 4

Take Charge of Your Debts

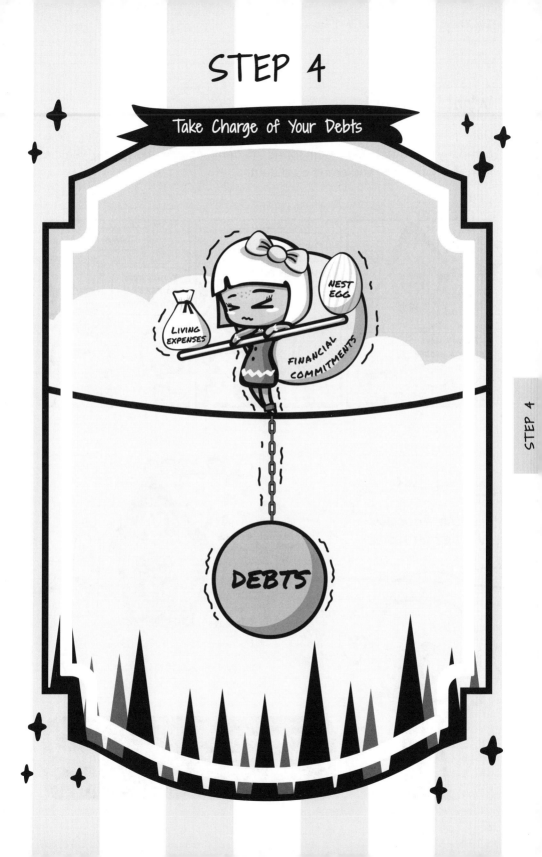

What is debt?

Debt is money borrowed from an individual, a financial institution or a company (creditor). Common forms of debt include mortgage, vehicle loan, personal loan and credit card debt.

INSTALMENT

People take loans to finance big-ticket purchases. Most loans are to be repaid regularly with scheduled payments (instalments) over a mutually agreed duration. Every instalment consists of a portion of the principal borrowed and the interest on the loan.

DOWN PAYMENT

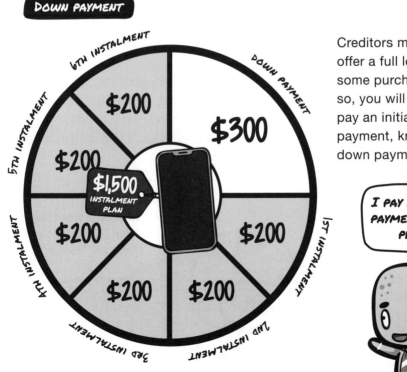

Creditors might not offer a full loan for some purchases. If so, you will need to pay an initial partial payment, known as down payment.

I PAY A SMALL DOWN PAYMENT TO OWN THE PHONE NOW.

STEP 4

83

THE TRUE VALUE OF YOUR PURCHASE

When you buy a computer with cash for $2,000, the purchase value is $2,000. However, if you take a loan to buy the computer, the purchase value is $2,000 plus interest. The same computer costs more when you take a loan! Creditors make money by charging interest on the loans they offer.

Be prudent about borrowing money

A loan is a financial commitment. You are legally obliged to repay the loan.

WHEN TO TAKE A LOAN

You might need to borrow money at some stage in your life, perhaps to fund your university education or buy your first home. Some people however take loans for daily expenses or even to pay for a holiday; that's not a wise move. Do not apply for a loan mindlessly just because you want something badly and do not have the money to buy it.

If you must take a loan, make sure it's for the right reasons and you can repay the loan punctually and in full. Here are three things to keep in mind.

1

Take a loan only for **needs**, not **wants**.

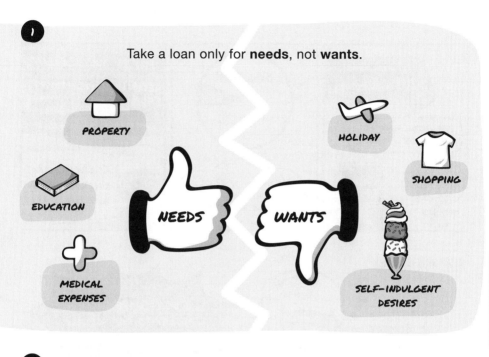

2

Take a loan only if you are confident that you can repay the loan after **deducting your living expenses**.

STEP 4

85

3 Take a loan only if you know you won't be overstretching yourself financially. Be mindful of your **total debt**.

COMPARING LOANS

Do your research before you take a loan. Do not be enticed by promotions or fanciful marketing brochures and smooth sales pitches. You need to make *informed decisions* based on your circumstances — the best deal for your friends might not be the right one for you.

Financial institutions, such as banks and credit card companies, update their loan rates and fees regularly according to market conditions. Search their websites to get the latest rates. Read the fine print too.

Scan here to calculate your estimated monthly repayment amount.

BANK A

INTEREST	PROCESSING FEE
2.68% P.A	5%

MAXIMUM LOAN
5X YOUR SALARY

MAXIMUM LOAN TENURE
1 YEAR

BANK B

INTEREST	PROCESSING FEE
3.88% P.A	1%

MAXIMUM LOAN
3X YOUR SALARY

MAXIMUM LOAN TENURE
2 YEARS

BANK C

INTEREST	PROCESSING FEE
3.68% P.A	2%

MAXIMUM LOAN
4X YOUR SALARY

MAXIMUM LOAN TENURE
3 YEARS

STEP 4

MAXIMUM LOAN TENURE

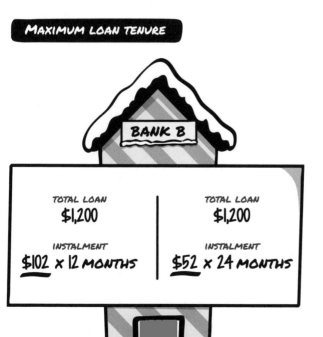

BANK B

TOTAL LOAN
$1,200

INSTALMENT
$102 x 12 MONTHS

TOTAL LOAN
$1,200

INSTALMENT
$52 x 24 MONTHS

Maximum loan tenure is the maximum amount of time you are given to repay a loan. The duration varies depending on the financial institution's policy. The longer the loan tenure, the lower the monthly instalments.

87

Paying a lower monthly instalment means you have more money every month for other things in life. However, it is better to keep the loan tenure as short as possible. When the loan tenure is longer, the total amount that you end up paying is higher.

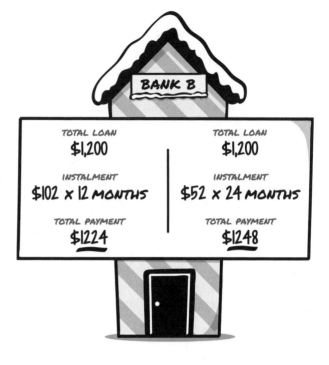

MAXIMUM LOAN

There is a limit to how much you can borrow from financial institutions. Typically, the maximum loan limit is based on your annual income to ensure that you don't overstretch yourself.

BANK
**LOAN UP TO
5x YOUR SALARY**

EASY CREDIT
**LOAN UP TO
20x YOUR SALARY**

Because of loan limits, some people turn to illegal moneylenders to borrow the amount they want. Illegal moneylenders are willing to loan more, but their interest rates are excessively high.

Those who borrow from illegal moneylenders pay exorbitant interest. The interest can even accumulate to be more than the actual loan! Illegal moneylenders are unscrupulous; they won't think twice about harassing their borrowers who miss the instalments. It's no surprise they are called loan sharks. Never borrow from illegal moneylenders!

STEP 4

89

LATE PAYMENT FEE

You are legally responsible for the timely repayment of your loan. A late payment fee is charged when your payment is overdue. Late payment fees are unnecessary expenses and will affect your credit score. Be disciplined! Do not miss your payment date.

CREDIT SCORE

A credit score is a number that represents a person's creditworthiness. The score is based on information sourced from credit bureaus. Recent loans, bad debts and late credit card payment will negatively affect your credit score.

Financial institutions and credit card companies use credit scores to identify potential risk, that is, how likely a debtor will repay their debts. In most cases, a person with a bad credit score would not be able to qualify for a loan or credit card. Even if approved, they might need to pay a higher interest rate or have their credit card limits reduced.

STEP 4

Refinancing

Refinancing is the replacement of an existing loan with another loan under different terms. There are two reasons why you should refinance your loan.

To get a better deal
Changing market conditions affect interest rates. You refinance to save money when interest rates fall.

OLD LOAN
3% INTEREST

INSTALMENT
$965.61 x 120 MONTHS

TOTAL PAYABLE
$115,873.20

NEW LOAN
3% INTEREST

INSTALMENT
$1,796.87 x 60 MONTHS

LEGAL FEE
$1,500

TOTAL PAYABLE
$109,312.14

COST SAVINGS
$6,561.06

Furthermore, as you move up the career ladder, you will have more disposable income. You can refinance to set a shorter loan tenure to save money on the total interest paid.

To reduce the monthly instalment
A long-term illness or prolonged economic downturn will reduce your monthly income. In such times, you can refinance to reduce your monthly instalment. But note that this is done at the expense of paying more interest.

OLD LOAN
3% INTEREST

INSTALMENT
$965.61 x 120 MONTHS

TOTAL PAYABLE
$115,873.20

NEW LOAN
3% INTEREST

INSTALMENT
$554.60 x 240 MONTHS

LEGAL FEE
$1,500

TOTAL PAYABLE
$134,604

FINANCIAL COMMITMENTS

ADDITIONAL COST
$18,730.80

GOOD TO KNOW

You can refinance your loan through your current lender
or bring your debt to a new financial institution.

Financial institutions typically charge a legal fee
when you refinance your loan. Remember to
consider this additional cost.

Some loans have a lock-in period with a guaranteed lower interest rate. There will be a penalty if you cancel or pay off the loan during this period.

Credit and debit cards

Credit and debit cards are payment tools issued by financial institutions which let cardholders pay for goods and services. Both cards offer convenience because you don't need to carry cash and coins.

CREDIT CARDS

When you purchase goods and services using your credit card, the amount spent is added to your credit limit. Your annual income determines your credit limit — the more you earn, the higher the limit. You cannot spend more than your credit limit. Credit card companies give their customers 15 to 30 days to pay the outstanding balance.

STEP 4

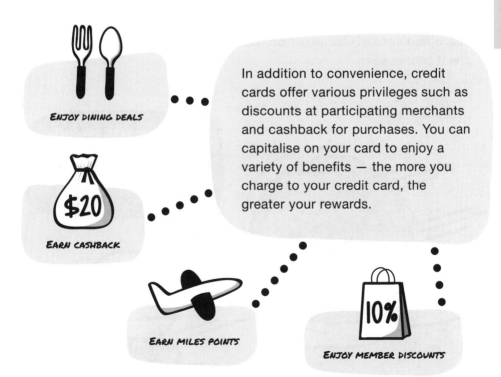

ENJOY DINING DEALS

EARN CASHBACK

In addition to convenience, credit cards offer various privileges such as discounts at participating merchants and cashback for purchases. You can capitalise on your card to enjoy a variety of benefits — the more you charge to your credit card, the greater your rewards.

EARN MILES POINTS

ENJOY MEMBER DISCOUNTS

But remember that your credit card is a means of payment. It should not be used as a borrowing tool (credit line). It is easy to spend unnecessarily or overspend when you have a credit line. It is very easy to fall into the credit card debt trap.

Practise self-discipline and make sure you have the money to pay for what you have bought with your credit card. The credit card company charges interest to customers who fail to pay the balance in full after the payment due date. You need to pay off your credit purchases **on time** to avoid the **exorbitant** interest charge, which can wipe out any cost savings from your credit card rewards.

BUY NOW, PAY NOW

I THINK I HAVE ENOUGH MONEY IN MY BANK ACCOUNT.

CASHIER

DEBIT CARD

DEBIT CARDS

Unlike credit cards, debit cards have no credit lines and are ideal for people who lack self-control but want the convenience of cashless payment. When you use a debit card, the money will be deducted immediately from your bank account.

Debit cards have fewer privileges compared to credit cards. You might still enjoy discounts at participating merchants, but the overall benefits are usually negligible.

STEP 4

THE RIGHT CARD FOR YOU

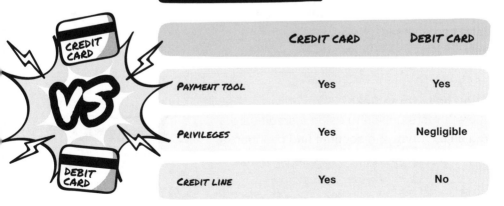

CREDIT CARD

DEBIT CARD

	CREDIT CARD	DEBIT CARD
PAYMENT TOOL	Yes	Yes
PRIVILEGES	Yes	Negligible
CREDIT LINE	Yes	No

97

Checklist ✅

Complete the checklist below to find the right card for you. Tick the box if the sentence is correct.

☐ Do you tend to **spend less** than you can afford?

☐ Have you built your **emergency fund**?

☐ Do you pay your bills **on time**?

If you have fewer than three ticks
It's not wise for you to use a credit card as you will be exposed to high interest charges. Use a debit card instead.

If you have three ticks
There is more upside to using a credit card. You enjoy rebates, discounts and cashbacks. Remember to pay your credit card bill on time.

COMPARING CARDS

There are many credit and debit cards on the market. Compare the different cards to see what best suits you and to get the best deal.

1. Compare cards from different companies

2. Evaluate your spending habits

3. Choose the card with privileges or rewards that complement your needs

Getting out of debt

Life is unpredictable and unexpected things can happen. In such times, you may need to take a large emergency loan to see you through the crisis. Be aware that this can get you into debt.

If you are overwhelmed with debt, the first thing you must do is change your spending habits. Prioritise all efforts to repay the debt even if you have to live on bread and water.

You can try to negotiate with your creditors and work out a repayment plan. Creditors might agree to reduce the instalment amount and increase the loan tenure, but you will likely have to pay more over time.

You can approach government agencies for assistance. Some countries have social service agencies that provide personalised financial advice. In Singapore, the Credit Counselling Singapore (CCS) works with creditors to help borrowers manage repayments within their payment capacity. Borrowers can also avoid legal actions from creditors with the intervention of the CCS.

Stop the time bomb ticking away! When you are stuck in debt, you must take decisive actions to get out of it. Failing to do so will result in bankruptcy.

Bankruptcy

If you go bankrupt, it means you are unable to pay off your outstanding debts. You will be forced to sell your possessions to clear the debt.

WHAT HAPPENS AFTER YOU ARE DECLARED A BANKRUPT?

Your existing assets and investments will be sold.

Your credit score will be badly affected.

You will have difficulty finding jobs that require you to handle money, such as finance and banking related jobs.

You will have difficulty applying for new loans and credit cards.

You will not be allowed to leave the country without a valid reason and official approval.

Your expenses will be monitored by a tax officer.

You must work to repay your creditors until you are discharged.

But note that creditors cannot hound you for payment while you are bankrupt.

GOOD TO KNOW

Bankruptcy is not the end of the world. In fact, the bankruptcy process is designed to help you get relief from your debtors and create a plan to repay your debts. You can be discharged from bankruptcy after paying off all outstanding debts or after a certain period. Every country has its own bankruptcy laws.

I'M BANKRUPT.

THREE YEARS LATER

INSOLVENCY OFFICE

BANKRUPT

PRAY MY CASE IS APPROVED.

In Singapore, a review and assessment will be conducted by the Official Assignee after three years in bankruptcy.

BE RESPONSIBLE

Filing for bankruptcy can lead to loss of self-esteem and confidence as well as depression. Do not let yourself get into such a situation. Practise good financial habits and self-discipline.

STEP 4

STUDIOUS
PERSISTENT
DILIGENT
KIND
DEDICATED
MINDFUL

IMPULSIVE
SPENDTHRIFT
IRRESPONSIBLE

SELF-DISCIPLINE

GOOD FINANCIAL HABITS

TL;DR

1. Purchases made with a loan might end up costing more.

2. You are legally responsible for the timely repayment of your loan.

3. Use a debit card if you have poor financial habits and lack self-discipline.

4. Prioritise and manage your debt to avoid bankruptcy.

YOU ARE RESPONSIBLE FOR THE CHOICES YOU MAKE

STEP 5

What is investment?

An investment is an asset purchased to generate income or to resell at a higher price. Examples of assets include property, stocks, insurance, even precious metals such as gold. There are many types of investment, with different rates of returns and investment risk.

Be careful with what you invest in to reduce risk and maximise returns. As always, you need to make *informed decisions*.

Why you need to invest

You invest to supplement your salary income and build your retirement fund. It is not enough to rely on savings alone. The good news is, if you start investing early and build a portfolio of reliable investments, you can have a steady stream of income for your retirement years.

STEP 5

Investing is time-rewarding. The longer you invest, the more you benefit from the power of compounding. You will also be better protected against market downturns and investment volatility, where asset prices are unpredictable and change very quickly.

107

COMPOUND INTEREST

Compound interest means "interest on interest". Instead of withdrawing the interest earned, you reinvest the interest to earn more money.

Smart investors use compound interest to grow their retirement fund. Compound interest grows exponentially over time. The earlier you invest, the more money you earn! Avoid withdrawing unnecessarily from your investment account as doing so will affect the compounding effect.

SAVING VS INVESTING

A penny saved is a penny earned. But instead of leaving your money in your piggy bank (no interest) or a savings account (low interest), invest your money in reliable products to earn higher interest. At the same time, do not neglect your emergency fund (see Step 2). You can only focus on your investments when your current financial well-being is secure.

Gambling, investing, speculating

Gambling and investing involve risk, but they are worlds apart. With gambling, you do not own anything, and you either win or lose money after the bet is over. With investing, you own the assets you bought, and you can choose when you want to sell.

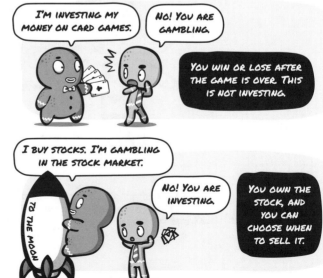

THE RETURNS LOOK ATTRACTIVE. I CAN EARN UP TO 100% OF MY INVESTMENT.

HIGH-RISK INVESTMENT

Speculating means investing in the hope of gaining profit and is often done at great risk. If you lose money, you might not recover your losses over time. Speculating is not gambling. Gambling is a game of chance while speculating involves research and calculated risk. With due diligence, the probability of gaining profit from speculating is much higher than from gambling.

THIS INVESTMENT IS QUITE RISKY. I RISK LOSING UP TO 50% OF MY INVESTMENT.

EPS

DEBT

PE RATIO

PEG RATIO

I HAVE THE CAPACITY IN MY PORTFOLIO TO TAKE ON SOME RISK.

INVESTMENT PORTFOLIO

RISKY

SAFE

I'LL ADD THIS INVESTMENT TO MY PORTFOLIO.

STEP 5

The Greater Fool Theory

Ever wonder why people buy assets with no intrinsic value at a ridiculously high price? The greater fool theory argues that prices are high because there are "fools" who are willing to speculate regardless of the asset's intrinsic value. The "fool" then resells the asset at a profit to a "greater fool". This cycle continues until there are no more buyers. Finally, the "greatest fool" will hold on to a worthless asset that no one wants to buy.

I FOUND AN INTERESTING COIN ON THE FLOOR

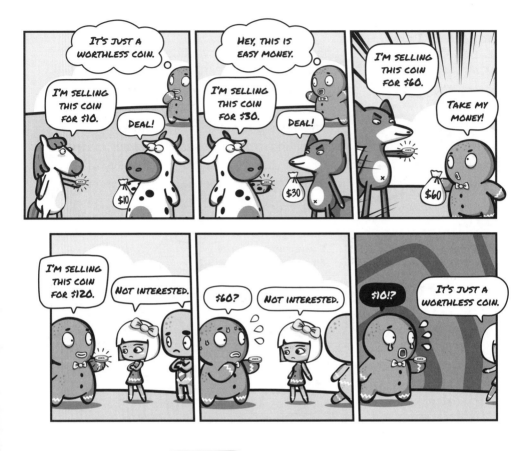

FOR ASSETS WITH NO INTRINSIC VALUE, SOMEONE HAS TO LOSE MONEY IN ORDER FOR OTHERS TO PROFIT.

You can minimise investment risk

Investing in assets that rely solely on timing and momentum is very risky, even if you have learnt how to interpret market data and can identify trends. While it is possible to make a quick profit, you might end up with significant losses.

All investments involve some degree of risk and there is the potential to lose your hard-earned money. Do not invest blindly, do not listen to hearsay. Do your research to manage investment risk and avoid unnecessary losses.

There are three strategies to help you minimise investment risk. We show you how on the following pages.

STEP 5

113

Do not let your investments affect your financial well-being or derail your plans to build your retirement fund. Only invest with money that you have budgeted for, and do not borrow recklessly. As always, question the assumptions you make.

Some people are impulsive and allow their emotions to rule their investment decisions. They greedily buy at a high price when the market is soaring and fearfully sell at a loss when the market is falling. Emotions can overpower rational thinking and lead to bad decision making.

2. BUILD A DIVERSIFIED PORTFOLIO

Since investments carry risk, you should try to minimise the risk of financial loss. You can reduce risk by building a diversified portfolio, one that spreads across different industries (such as healthcare, technology or utilities) and asset classes (such as stocks, fixed deposits or real estate).

STEP 5

115

If one of your investments performs poorly, the impact won't badly affect your portfolio. In other words, don't put all your eggs in one basket.

There are two common asset allocation strategies to build a diversified portfolio and balance risk.

2A You allocate money into each asset class based on your risk appetite. This is called **strategic asset allocation**. The value of each asset will change over time. You will then rebalance the allocation periodically back to the initial settings.

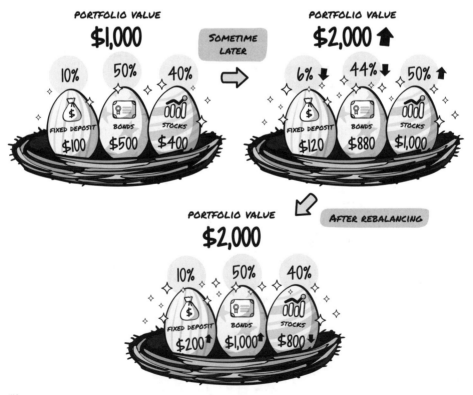

2B You allocate money based on market trends and economic conditions. This is called **tactical asset allocation**.

STEP 5

STRATEGIC ASSET ALLOCATION VS TACTICAL ASSET ALLOCATION

	STRATEGIC	**TACTICAL**
INVESTMENT VIEW	Long term	Short to mid-term
EFFORT REQUIRED	**Minimal** *You create a plan once and rebalance it periodically.*	**Time-consuming** *You need to monitor the market actively.*
CONS	*You will not be able to take advantage of favourable opportunities.*	*You need discipline to avoid making emotional decisions, and skills and luck to time the market.*

3. USE DOLLAR-COST AVERAGING

Generally, you will want to buy when the price is low and sell when the price is high. But the reality is that no one can accurately predict the market conditions. It is hard to determine whether the price will keep dropping or will rise any higher. Timing the market is not a good idea.

However, you can reduce the risk of entering the market at the "wrong" time by using the Dollar-Cost Averaging investment strategy. In this strategy, you invest a fixed sum of money at predetermined intervals, whether the market is up or down on that day.

NEWS FLASH: WATER COMPANY FILES FOR BANKRUPTCY PROTECTION

I SHOULDN'T HAVE USED DOLLAR-COST AVERAGING. NOW I'VE LOST ALL MY MONEY.

You use dollar-cost averaging based on the assumption that prices will eventually go up. This strategy works best on safe asset classes such as blue-chip stocks and exchange-traded funds (ETF).

Even then, you should not invest in a declining company that has little chance of recovery. You might end up losing even more money.

Investing 101

Learning to invest is essential — do not jump in blindly and make impulse decisions with your money. The chart below gives an overview of the different asset classes and their risk profile; use it as a reference as you start to learn more about investing. The worksheets that follow will help you gain a better understanding of what is required of you before you plunge into investing.

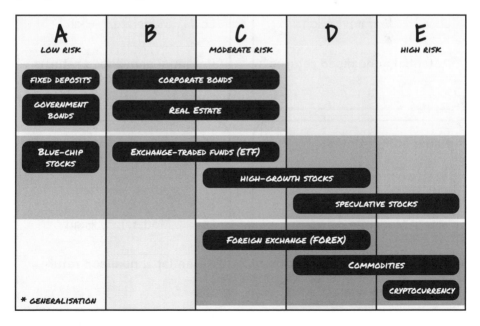

A LOW RISK	B	C MODERATE RISK	D	E HIGH RISK
FIXED DEPOSITS	CORPORATE BONDS			
GOVERNMENT BONDS	REAL ESTATE			
BLUE-CHIP STOCKS	EXCHANGE-TRADED FUNDS (ETF)			
		HIGH-GROWTH STOCKS		
			SPECULATIVE STOCKS	
		FOREIGN EXCHANGE (FOREX)		
			COMMODITIES	
				CRYPTOCURRENCY

* GENERALISATION

STEP 5

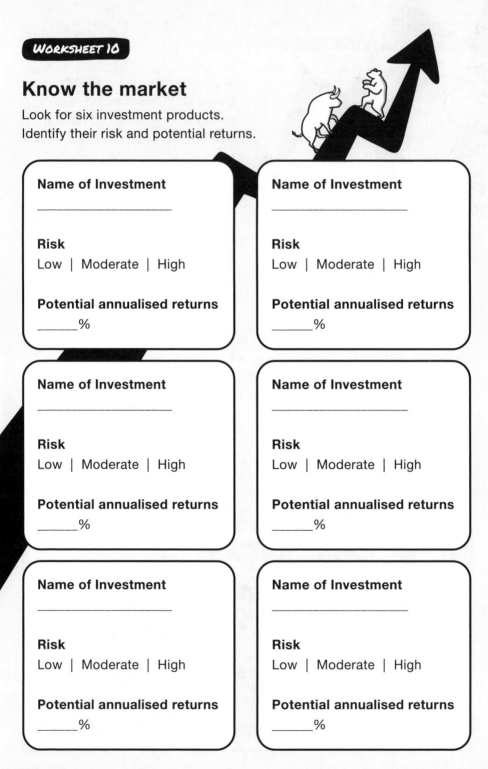

WORKSHEET 10

Know the market

Look for six investment products.
Identify their risk and potential returns.

Name of Investment

_____

Risk
Low | Moderate | High

Potential annualised returns
_____%

Name of Investment

_____

Risk
Low | Moderate | High

Potential annualised returns
_____%

Name of Investment

_____

Risk
Low | Moderate | High

Potential annualised returns
_____%

Name of Investment

_____

Risk
Low | Moderate | High

Potential annualised returns
_____%

Name of Investment

_____

Risk
Low | Moderate | High

Potential annualised returns
_____%

Name of Investment

_____

Risk
Low | Moderate | High

Potential annualised returns
_____%

WORKSHEET 11

a) Know your risk profile

How much risk are you willing to take (risk appetite)? What is the acceptable level of losses you are willing to bear (risk tolerance)?

SAFE

LOW RISK
100%

STRATEGIC ASSET ALLOCATION

CAUTIOUS

LOW RISK
80%

MODERATE TO HIGH RISK
20%

STRATEGIC ASSET ALLOCATION

ADVENTUROUS

LOW RISK
60%

MODERATE TO HIGH RISK
40%

TACTICAL ASSET ALLOCATION

Tick the box that best describes you.

Safe
I want to avoid losing money. The returns will be minimal.

Cautious
I am prepared to lose up to 20% of my capital in hope of some potential returns over time.

Adventurous
I am prepared to lose 21–40% of my capital to achieve high potential returns over time.

STEP 5

b) Identify your investment goals

Set your goals based on your risk profile. Your goals must be realistic, specific and achievable.

Scan here for our investment calculator to find out if your goal is realistic.

1) I want to earn $_____ investment income annually by _____ (year).

2) I want to have an investment portfolio worth $_____ by _____ (year).

GOAL

Research before you buy

Investing without adequate research is akin to shooting a target in the dark. You need to do your homework to increase the chances of choosing the right investment to grow your money. The more you know, the better the decisions you can make.

BUY THESE GEMS AND GET RICH!

DO RESEARCH TO AVOID INVESTING IN OVERPRICED ASSETS OR SCAMS.

WHAT TO LOOK OUT FOR

STOCKS / BONDS

FINANCIAL STATUS

FUTURE PROSPECTS

COMPETITORS

FIXED DEPOSITS

INTEREST RATES

TERMS AND CONDITIONS

TENURE

PROPERTY

MARKET TRENDS

LOCATION

RENTAL YIELD

PROPERTY CONDITION

AVOID FOLLOWING THE CROWD WHEN MAKING INVESTMENT DECISIONS. RESEARCH BEFORE YOU INVEST.

DIAMOND HANDS.

BUY AND HOLD. WE ARE GOING TO THE MOON!

BUY NOW! SHORT SQUEEZE COMING.

I SHOULDN'T INVEST BLINDLY.

If you feel overwhelmed with the time, skills and effort required for investing, you can seek professional help to create and execute your investment plan.

CONSULT A PROFESSIONAL FINANCIAL ADVISER WITH A PROVEN TRACK RECORD.

USE A ROBO-ADVISOR TO MANAGE YOUR INVESTMENTS.

Stick to your plan

It takes time for your investment to grow. Do not worry about short-term volatility as market ups and downs are part of investing. Manage your investment risk and practise dollar-cost averaging. You created a plan to keep emotions out of investing, so stick to the plan!

TAKE NOTE!
Profits from your investment should be allocated back into your investment funds. Avoid the temptation to spend the profits. Practise delayed gratification.

STEP 5

Investment scams

Investment scams are fraudulent schemes that deceive investors to part with their money. Scammers lure unsuspecting investors with the promise of a great financial opportunity. Unfortunately, investors often lose all their money without hope of recouping their losses.

THE PONZI SCHEME

One of the largest investment scams in history is the Ponzi scheme run by Bernard Madoff in 2008. Thousands of investors were defrauded by the American financier, and losses were estimated to be US$65 billion.

The Ponzi scheme lures investors with the promise of low risk and high profit. Investors are sold the big lie that their profit comes from legitimate investments. Instead, the earlier investors are paid using money collected from newer investors. A Ponzi scheme can last for years until the number of new investors slows down and the scammers can no longer pay the promised returns.

PUMP-AND-DUMP SCHEME

Pump-and-dump is an old scheme out in the news again with the rise of online chat groups and internet forums. Scammers attempt to artificially inflate the price of their assets (pump) through false or exaggerated statements to unsuspecting investors. Once the price rises, the scammers sell their assets all at once (dump). This action will cause the price to drop dramatically, leaving the new investors stuck with the overpriced assets.

STEP 5

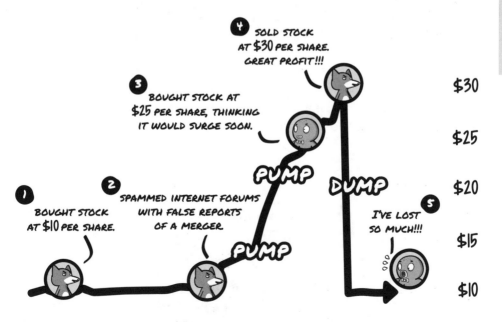

HOW TO SPOT AN INVESTMENT SCAM

Investment scams can happen to anyone. You need to be vigilant and keep a lookout for signs of a scam, such as too-good-to-be-true promises of high returns, insider news that cannot be verified and inflated claims of worthiness of a product.

Theranos Inc, a US healthcare technology start-up, raised over US$700 million from investors to develop and distribute their blood-testing device. Its CEO claimed the device could run hundreds of tests from just one pinprick of blood taken from the finger. However, in 2016, medical authorities revealed that the claims were false and people's health had been put at risk. Theranos closed in 2017 and investors lost their money.

Money lost through investment scams is often unrecoverable. Do not be tempted by promises of high returns or pressured into making an investment. Do your research and think twice before you sign on the dotted line! If a deal looks too good to be true, it probably is too good to be true.

HOW TO PROTECT YOURSELF FROM INVESTMENT SCAMS

IGNORE UNSOLICITED OFFERS TO INVEST

DO YOUR DUE DILIGENCE

ASK QUESTIONS

USE CRITICAL THINKING

STEP 5

TL;DR

1. Invest to build your retirement nest egg.

2. All investments carry some degree of risk.

3. Build a diversified portfolio.

4. Don't succumb to greed and fear.

5. Learn to spot and protect yourself from investment scams.

STEP 6

Take Charge of Your Future

GREAT MISFORTUNE

SMALL MISFORTUNE

GREAT BLESSING

大吉

Change is the only constant

Did you know the first smartphone was sold in 1994 and was called Simon the Personal Communicator? Compared with today's smartphones, it was a simple device with limited functions. Smartphones have since changed the way people work and consume information. Automation has impacted the human workplace since the Industrial Revolution. Emerging technologies like Artificial Intelligence and Machine Learning will continue to transform the way we work, play and live. While life is full of uncertainty, change is the only constant.

PREDICT THE UNPREDICTABLE

The future is unpredictable. Accidents and illnesses, retrenchment or unexpected financial losses can significantly impact your financial well-being. While many things are beyond your control, it is within your power to be prepared — and make *informed decisions* to safeguard your future.

Plan your life

Your financial needs change at different points in your life. The responsibilities and monthly expenses of a fresh graduate are different from someone close to retirement. You can predict your financial needs at various life stages to define your financial goals and priorities. Here is a simple roadmap of these stages and their respective financial considerations.

STEP 6

STAGE 1: HITTING THE BOOKS

As a student, your priority is to acquire knowledge and learn new skills. You go to school, but getting an education is more than just passing exams; it is to help you jumpstart your career.

Having the right set of qualifications, both tertiary and professional, will open more job opportunities and increase your income potential. Education is costly but it is a meaningful investment that will benefit you throughout your life.

Find out the fees and start saving for it.

If you take a loan, you must be prepared to set aside money to repay the loan once you graduate and have a job.

STAGE 2: ENTERING THE WORKFORCE

You've completed formal studies and have secured a job. Your priorities are twofold: to save and to have insurance coverage. Savings and insurance are important regardless of whether you choose to remain single or get married and start a family.

Save, save, save
You will receive a salary once you start working. Resist the urge to splurge! Make a concerted effort to save and be disciplined about it.

You save by not spending on unnecessary things now to be able to spend on what you might need in the future. Having money will see you through difficult times and help you avoid having to make bad money decisions.

Buy insurance

Insurance is a contract that protects you from financial losses. You set aside money from your salary income to buy insurance and pay the premiums.

There are three main types of insurances: general insurance, health insurance and life insurance.

STEP 6

General insurance protects you from personal financial losses and damage to your assets caused by unforeseen circumstances. General insurance gives you a sense of security by covering for the unexpected.

CAR INSURANCE

FIRE INSURANCE

TRAVEL INSURANCE

Health insurance protects you from the high cost of healthcare treatment. Buy health insurance when you are healthy to protect yourself when you are sick. Get covered in case you need to be hospitalised or develop a chronic ailment that requires long-term treatment.

CRITICAL ILLNESS INSURANCE

DISABILITY INSURANCE

PERSONAL ACCIDENT INSURANCE

INVESTMENT-LINKED
INSURANCE

SAVINGS
INSURANCE

TERM LIFE
INSURANCE

WHOLE LIFE
INSURANCE

Life insurance protects you from financial hardship after you retire. Note that some investment-linked insurance products carry risk, and you might lose your money. Read the fine print carefully before buying such insurance.

Life insurance also protects your family from financial hardship in the event of your death or permanent disability.

While life insurance is a long-term commitment, it offers peace of mind. It is good to purchase life insurance once you start working as the premiums are lower when you are young and healthy. Start early!

STEP 6

TAKE NOTE!
Avoid going to the extreme and overinsuring yourself. You do not want to waste money on unnecessary insurance when the money could be used for investments. Do your financial profiling or approach a professional financial planner before buying any insurance.

STAGE 3: ESTABLISHING YOURSELF – THE MID-CAREER YEARS

At this stage, you have gained much experience career-wise and will begin to take on leadership roles. You should continue to develop yourself professionally. With every promotion, you earn a higher salary.

Your priority would be to build a reliable cash flow and have an emergency fund covering at least six months' worth of expenses. Focus on clearing all debts.

Your monthly income should be consistently higher than your expenses. If you have not done so, you should start to invest a small sum of money regularly to grow your investment portfolio.

Achieving financial freedom means you have complete control over your finances and can make financial decisions without worrying about the next bill.

STAGE 4: PREPARING FOR RETIREMENT

It's never too early to prepare for your retirement years and start to grow your nest egg.

A nest egg is a sum of money or a pool of assets accumulated for a specific purpose, in this case, retirement. You stop drawing a salary when you retire, but your bills do not stop. A substantial nest egg will provide financial security, cover your retirement expenses and give you peace of mind.

STEP 6

You grow your nest egg with savings and regular investments throughout your working years. At this stage of your life, you should see the compounding effects of your investments. Continue to accumulate your wealth by allocating money into investments. You might want to avoid high-risk investment as you have less time to recover from losses.

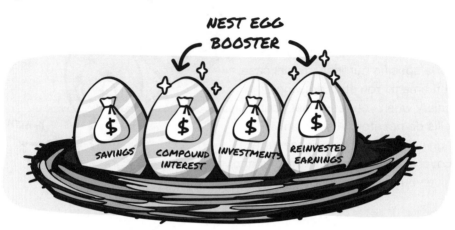

Your quality of life after retirement depends on the financial choices you make before you retire. Manage your spending, save for emergencies and invest wisely!

STAGE 5: LIVING FULLY – THE RETIREMENT YEARS

It's time to enjoy the fruits of your labour! Create a spending plan based on your lifestyle and inflation (more on inflation in the next section). Set aside money for out-of-pocket medical expenses that are not covered by your insurance. You can consider investing a portion of your nest egg on safe assets such as bonds or fixed deposits. Your nest egg should be sufficient to cover your living expenses if you have been diligently saving and investing your money wisely.

Scan here to calculate how much you will need for retirement.

Be prepared for economic downturns

Throughout your life, you will experience ups and downs in the economy. When times are good, job opportunities are abundant. When times are bad, companies start retrenching and the stock market turns bearish. This is known as the Economic Cycle.

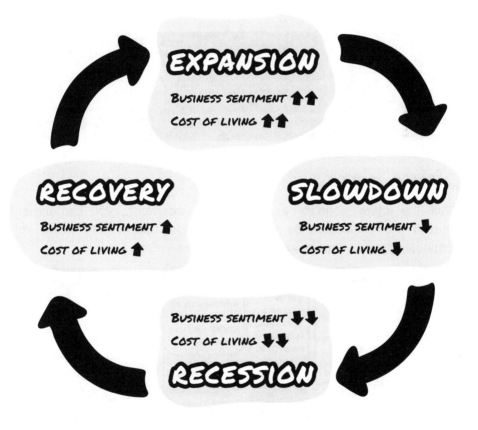

The economy travels through cycles — of recovery, expansion, slowdown and recession. You can make better financial decisions for the future when you understand how the economy moves through these periods.

A recession is a period of widespread economic decline. During a downturn, business revenues drop due to lower trade and industrial activity. Companies start retrenching staff to reduce cost; those that incur severe losses might close for good. Prepare yourself before recession hits by having enough savings to tide you through tough times.

TAKE NOTE!

A depression is a more extreme economic downturn compared to recession. Recessions typically last for months but a depression can last for years. The Great Depression, which began in the US in 1929, spread through the whole world and lasted for ten years.

Lifelong learning

While the future world of work is full of uncertainty, you can protect yourself from recession by embracing lifelong learning in which you continually pursue knowledge and acquire new skills.

Enhancing your skill sets will make you more employable and help you remain relevant to your industry. In expanding your skill sets, you open up new career pathways and can take on new job opportunities when the economy rebounds.

WORKSHEET 12

What skill sets do I need?

Create a list of the skill sets you will need for your dream career.

HARD *SKILLS*	**SOFT** *SKILLS*

Create a list of skill sets that interest you.

HARD *SKILLS*	**SOFT** *SKILLS*

STEP 6

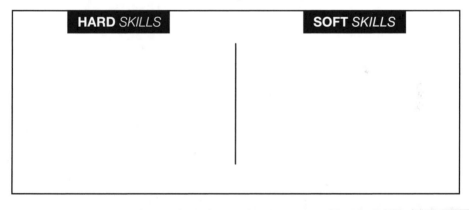

Investment opportunities in a recession

Business sentiment sinks during a recession. Stocks can fall by more than 30% and companies might even go bust. People who cannot pay their mortgage will be forced to sell their property at a low price.

> **I LOST MY JOB, MY CAR, MY HOUSE AND ALL MY SAVINGS.**

While falling asset prices will hurt your investment portfolio, it's possible to take advantage of the recession. The falling price is a buying opportunity that might bring substantial returns when the recession is over and the economy recovers.

Investing in a recession requires mental fortitude, patience and, most importantly, research to find out if the asset will emerge stronger during recovery.

INVESTMENT

GROW MY MONEY

> **MAKE SURE YOU ARE IN A STRONG FINANCIAL POSITION AND INVEST ONLY THE SURPLUS FUNDS THAT YOU HAVE BUDGETED FOR.**

PROPERTY PRICE INDEX

> **TAKE EMOTIONS OUT OF INVESTING. DON'T PANIC.**

STOCKS INDEX

> **DO NOT TIME THE MARKET*. INVEST FOR THE LONG TERM INSTEAD OF FOR SHORT-TERM GAINS.**

> **IS THE ASSET PRICE DOWN BECAUSE OF THE RECESSION, OR ARE THERE OTHER REASONS?**

LAND FOR SALE

* No one can foresee when the economy will hit bottom and how long it will take to recover.

Inflation and the purchasing power of money

The purchasing power of money is the amount of goods and services which you can buy with your money. As the economy grows and things get more expensive, your purchasing power falls; in other words, you get less for the same amount of money. The same goods and services you buy today will likely cost more in the future.

We know from historical data that inflation will undoubtedly go up, and the purchasing power of money will fall over time. Storing your money inside a savings account will reduce the value of your savings because the interest gained is often lower than the rate of inflation. You need to take inflation into account and make higher-interest investments to beat inflation.

What will happen to my $10,000 after ten years? Scan to find out.

INFLATION WILL EAT INTO YOUR SAVINGS. BEAT IT WITH SMART INVESTMENTS.

STEP 6

143

Protect your financial well-being in a digital world

Fintech, or financial technology, is transforming everyday life. Banks no longer need to have physical branch locations. You can simply send money to anyone or pay bills with your smartphone. The future is digital.

While fintech improves our financial lives and productivity, it also creates new risks that threaten to undermine our financial well-being. Two important areas to be careful with are password security and cyber theft. Be diligent about protecting yourself.

PASSWORD SECURITY

You secure your house with a lock to protect your assets and for privacy. In the digital world, your password is akin to a lock. A strong password will protect your personal data and prevent bad actors from stealing your financial assets.

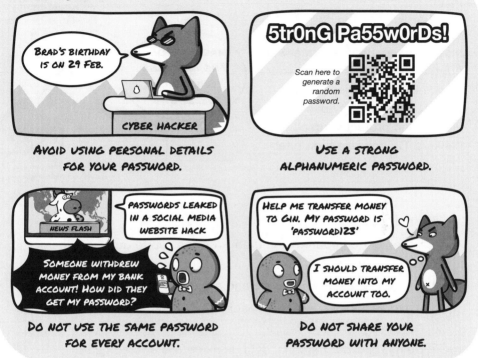

Most financial apps and websites support two-factor authentication, or 2FA. It is a security process that requires you to provide two different types of information (authentication factors) to gain access to your account.

STEP 6

Remember that 2FA is useless if your user account and email share the same password. Bad actors can simply log in to your email to retrieve the verification code.

CYBER THEFT

Every year, hackers steal billions from people around the world. You may have the strongest password, but it will be meaningless if your device is compromised or if you neglect cybersecurity basics. Be vigilant and protect yourself from hackers. Do not take their bite!

HACKING 101... THE IGNORANT ONES WILL SURELY BITE.

Protect yourself

- Keep your computers and mobile devices up to date with the latest security patch.
- Use anti-virus, anti-spyware and anti-malware software.
- Avoid suspicious websites, especially when making online purchases.
- Do not give out personal data, bank details or credit card numbers through emails.
- Be wary of emails and text messages sent over your smartphone.
- Do not click on any links. Beware of phishing and smishing.
- Do not use public Wi-Fi.

DIGITAL IDENTITY THEFT

Digital identity theft happens when someone uses another person's personal information without consent and misuses the information to commit crimes online.

Protect yourself

- Do not give out personal information.
- Use reputable websites or apps.
- If someone is desperate for money, verify the person's identity before transferring any money.

CALL THE PERSON YOURSELF.

ASK QUESTIONS THAT ONLY THE PERSON CAN ANSWER.

147

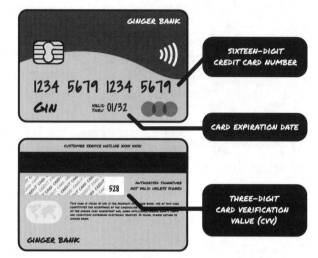

All credit cards have a sixteen-digit number, an expiration date and another three-digit code. Do not share your credit card information.

Set SMART goals

Everyone has dreams. Goal setting is a process that starts with a vision of yourself and then motivating yourself to turn your dream into reality. Having a long-term goal keeps you focused on that dream and allows you to progress towards your ideal future.

Once you have identified your long-term goal, you will need to create an action plan. The action plan consists of short-term goals for you to achieve on the way to reaching your long-term goal.

Make sure your goals are **SMART** goals: Specific, Measurable, Achievable, Realistic and Time-bound.

Then write out your Action Plan to achieve your SMART goals!

Planning for success

A long-term goal allows you to take charge of your life's direction. Short-term goals act as milestones to help you focus and determine whether you are on track to achieving your long-term goal.

☆ Action Plan

Today's date: **01 JAN 22**

◎ SHORT-TERM *GOAL*
complete ✓

OBTAIN A PART-TIME DEGREE IN BUSINESS MANAGEMENT

🕐 31 DEC 25

◎ SHORT-TERM *GOAL*
complete ✓

EARN A MONTHLY SALARY OF $5,000

🕐 31 DEC 30

◎ SHORT-TERM *GOAL*
complete ☐

SAVE $200,000 IN FIXED DEPOSIT ACCOUNT

🕐 31 DEC 35

◎ LONG-TERM *GOAL*
complete ☐

PURCHASE A CONDOMINIUM UNIT CLOSE TO TOWN

🕐 31 DEC 40

GOAL

STEP 6

WORKSHEET 13

Create your own action plan

Set milestones to achieve your long-term goal. Each goal should be specific, measurable, realistic and attainable within a timeline.

☆ **Action Plan**   Today's date: _____

◎ **SHORT-TERM** *GOAL*   complete ☐

◎ **SHORT-TERM** *GOAL*   complete ☐

◎ **SHORT-TERM** *GOAL*   complete ☐

◎ **LONG-TERM** *GOAL*   complete ☐

Your dreams will only come true if you work hard to achieve them. Motivate yourself to work towards the milestones and treat yourself when you accomplish a short-term goal. Success comes to those who work for it. Stay focused and never give up.

TL;DR

1. Define your financial goals and priorities at the different stages of your life.

2. The economy travels through predictable cycles. Use it to your advantage.

3. Beat inflation with investments.

4. Practise good digital habits.

5. Create an action plan to achieve your SMART goals.

STEP 6

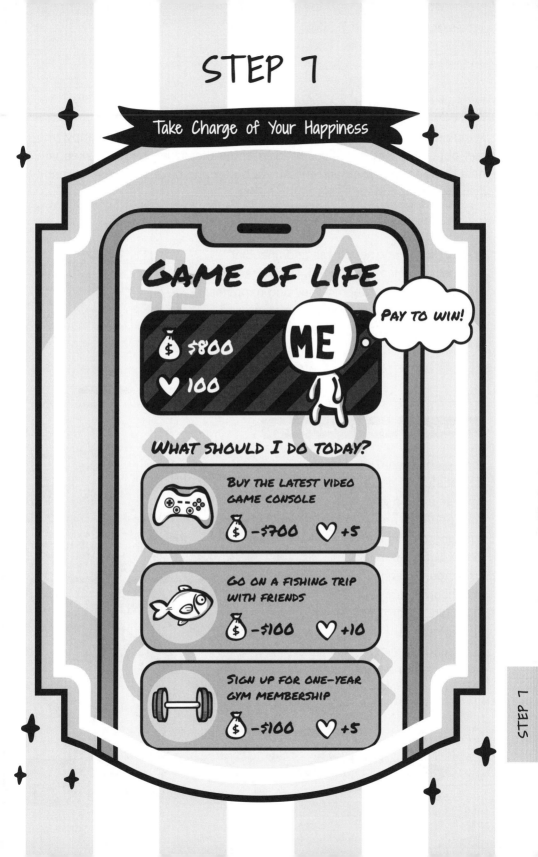

What is happiness?

Happiness is the emotional state of being happy. When you are happy, you feel contented and satisfied. Studies show that being happy makes you healthier because you deal with stress better and have a stronger immune system. You get to enjoy life to the fullest.

In today's society, happiness and financial well-being are interconnected. Understanding the relationship between money and happiness can help you make **_informed decisions_** and take charge of your happiness.

MONEY CAN PREVENT UNHAPPINESS

You've completed formal studies and have secured a job. Your priorities are twofold: to save and to have insurance coverage. Savings and insurance are important regardless of whether you choose to remain single or get married and start a family.

Having money puts you in a good financial position where you can make life choices that prioritise your happiness and keep you out of miserable situations. Plan your investments well, track them closely and take charge.

MONEY CAN BUY HAPPINESS BUT...

It's nice to buy things. We feel happy and satisfied when we have fulfilled the desire to spend, and excited when we own something new. While you can spend money to purchase things that make you happier, the happiness derived from spending usually is short-lived. In fact, spending more money doesn't always lead to more happiness. How you spend your money determines how much happier you will be.

How to spend and be happy

1. SPEND TO EXPERIENCE

You derive more happiness from experiential purchases than material purchases. The joy and memory of attending a concert or a baking class lasts for far longer than the happiness derived from buying things, which often fades quickly.

MEMORIES THAT LAST A LIFETIME!

HOLIDAY IN EGYPT   JUNGLE SAFARI   FISHING TRIP

Shared experiences with loved ones is priceless. The experiences not only strengthens relationships, the fond memories can be relived whenever you recall the experiences together.

GUITAR
$200

ENTRANCE FEE
$50

PARTICIPATION IN A TALENT COMPETITION WITH BESTIE
PRICELESS

GINGERTOWN GOT TALENT

2. SPEND TO SHARE

Instead of spending money on buying something for yourself, why not share the fruits of your labour with your loved ones or people who are facing financial hardship? Happiness obtained from bringing joy to others is very satisfying. Happiness shared is happiness doubled!

DINNER WITH LOVED ONES

ADVENTURE FOR TWO

FEED THE STRAYS

DONATE TO THOSE IN NEED

STEP 7

157

WORKSHEET 14

HAPPINESS X 2

The sharing list

Who will you share the fruits of your labour with?
Check the box when you have completed the task.

NAME ☐

What you want to do:

What it will cost:

NAME ☐

What you want to do:

What it will cost:

NAME ☐

What you want to do:

What it will cost:

NAME ☐

What you want to do:

What it will cost:

NAME ☐

What you want to do:

What it will cost:

NAME ☐

What you want to do:

What it will cost:

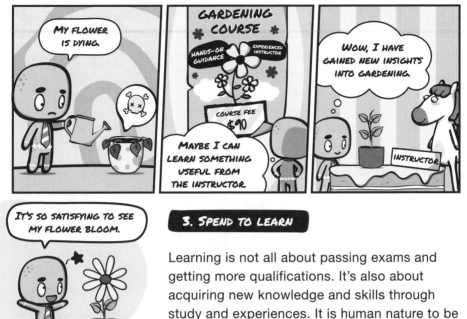

3. SPEND TO LEARN

Learning is not all about passing exams and getting more qualifications. It's also about acquiring new knowledge and skills through study and experiences. It is human nature to be curious. It's satisfying to learn something new and be able to share our interests with others.

There are many free courses and learning resources on the Internet. While any type of learning is good, there are benefits to paying for a course and learning from well-qualified and experienced instructors. The quality tends to be better and you learn more effectively.

STEP 7

159

4. Spend and be content

Being content means you are happy with what you have. This does not mean you should stop spending your money. Instead, you are grateful for what you have purchased and do not see the need to spend just to feel happy.

DO YOU KNOW THAT SOME CHILDREN CAN'T EVEN AFFORD A PAIR OF SCHOOL SHOES?

BE THANKFUL FOR WHAT YOU HAVE!

THE MOST POWERFUL PHONE EVER

PHONE 13

WE BOUGHT NEW PHONES.

SIX MONTHS LATER

PHONE 14

THE NEW MODEL IS OUT.

I MUST UPGRADE TO THE LATEST MODEL!

I'M CONTENT WITH MY CURRENT PHONE.

I SHOULD SAVE AND INVEST MY MONEY INSTEAD OF KEEPING UP WITH TRENDS.

SAVINGS

INVESTMENTS

Short-lived vs long-lasting happiness

What makes people happy is different for each person. Some obtain happiness from immediate gratification, when they spend money on fancy meals or buy new clothes. Others find happiness in building relationships and contributing to society. They prefer to spend money on their loved ones and donate to charity.

As you have seen, happiness can be short-lived. But happiness can also be long-lasting!

SHORT-LIVED HAPPINESS

- easy to obtain
- to satisfy one's own desires (self-gratification)

EATING A TUB
OF ICE CREAM

WATCHING A MOVIE

SHOPPING FOR
A NEW PHONE

GOING ON A
HOLIDAY

STEP 7

LONG-LASTING HAPPINESS

- harder to achieve
- springs from an inner sense of purpose to achieve one's life goals

DEDICATION TO A CAUSE

BUILDING MEANINGFUL RELATIONSHIPS

CONTRIBUTING BACK TO SOCIETY

BEING A MENTOR TO OTHERS

Those who have a clear purpose in life often achieve long-lasting happiness. They have something to strive for and are passionate about their goals. Long-lasting happiness requires effort and hard work. Having money makes the hard work easier.

Finding your purpose

To take charge of your happiness, you need to explore your interests and identify your purpose. Ask yourself: What will you do if you do not need to work for money?

Scan here to find out how you can make a difference in the world.

WORKSHEET 15

My Life Purpose Statement

Name

My life purpose

This drawing represents my life purpose

I PROMISE TO TAKE ACTIONS TO LIVE MY LIFE PURPOSE

_____ _____
Signature **Date**

It doesn't matter how much you spend. You will only find yourself trapped in a vicious cycle of chasing happiness if you do not understand the relationship between happiness and money. Consider our suggestions and change how you perceive happiness. Your happiness depends only on you.

TL;DR

1. Money can buy happiness but the happiness from spending is usually short-lived.

2. How you spend your money determines the type of happiness you get in return.

3. Having a sense of purpose from achieving life goals will lead to long-lasting happiness.

4. You are responsible for your own happiness.

5. The choice is yours!

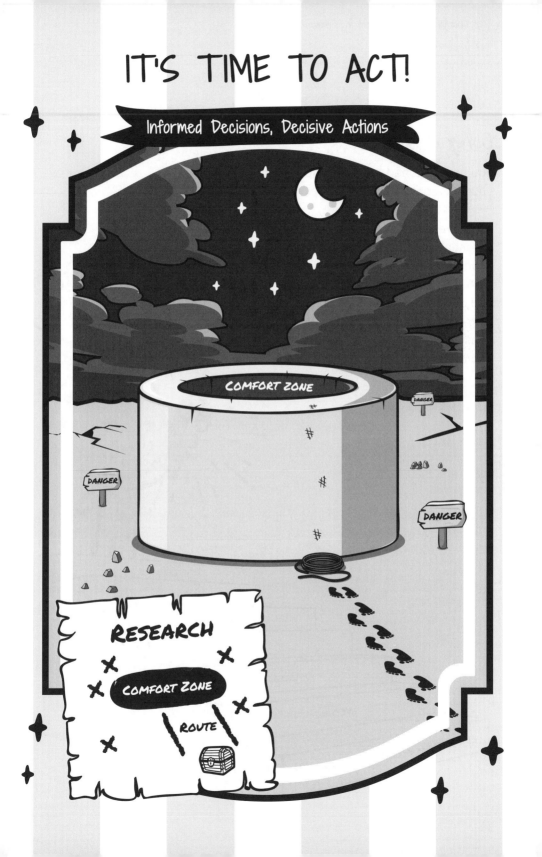

Congratulations!

You have reached the last chapter of this book. Give yourself a pat on the back!

You have learnt to increase your income potential (Steps 1 and 5), enhance your financial decision-making skills (Steps 2 to 4), safeguard your future (Step 6), and develop your own life goals to long-lasting happiness (Step 7). These seven steps will help you improve your financial well-being. It's now time to act!

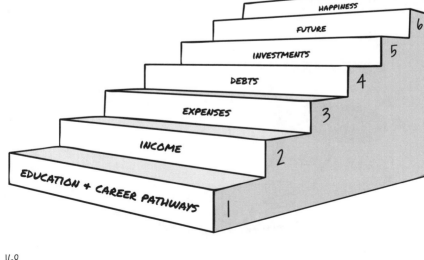

I LEARNT TO IMPROVE MY FINANCIAL WELL-BEING!

HAPPINESS 7

FUTURE 6

INVESTMENTS 5

DEBTS 4

EXPENSES 3

INCOME 2

EDUCATION + CAREER PATHWAYS 1

Make informed decisions

Life is full of choices. You make decisions every day. You decide what you eat, which shoes you will wear, which career path to take.

Now look back and think about the bad decisions you have made. Will you make the same mistakes again? I hope not! Wrong decisions are always in hindsight.

Throughout this book, we brought up the importance of making ***informed decisions*** — where decisions are based on facts and information. So, how do you go about it? Here are four easy steps.

GATHER RELEVANT INFORMATION

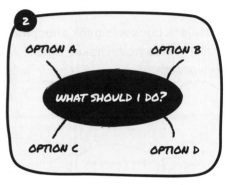

IDENTIFY ALTERNATIVES

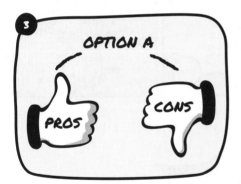

EVALUATE RISK AND POSSIBLE OUTCOMES
USING THE INFORMATION GATHERED

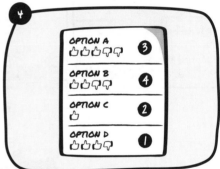

CREATE A PRIORITY LIST FROM THE
POSSIBLE ALTERNATIVES

Use the four steps whenever you have to make decisions. With facts and information as the basis, you will choose the best option available to you. Remember, the decisions you make will determine your future.

SELECT THE MOST FAVOURABLE
AMONG THE ALTERNATIVES

Take decisive actions

You have gained valuable knowledge and learnt to make **_informed decisions_**, but all these are useless if you don't act upon them. You need to apply what you have learnt!

Some people can motivate themselves constantly and act on their plans. They are willing to step out of their comfort zone to achieve their goals. For others, their motivation comes and goes.

So, how to start? First, set in motion your plan of action. Then strive to make each action a habit. For example, you have created a budget and decided how much money goes into each money jar; now you must intentionally follow through and stick to your budget plan. Set small goals and give yourself a treat when you have reached that goal. Once the habit is formed, the action will become second nature. Habits require little effort to maintain regardless of motivation.

SEVEN GOOD HABITS TO FORM

MAKE LEARNING A LIFELONG HABIT

DEVELOP A MONTHLY BUDGET PLAN

FIND OUT THE TRUE VALUE OF THE
PURCHASE BEFORE TAKING A LOAN

THINK BEFORE SPENDING

RESEARCH BEFORE INVESTING

KEEP YOUR DEVICES PATCHED
AND UP TO DATE

LIVE YOUR PURPOSE
EVERY DAY

The End

Thank you for taking the time to read this book. We hope the content and ideas will encourage you to take steps to improve your financial well-being. Do your research to make informed decisions and take decisive actions to achieve your goals. Be money smart — because the smart money decisions that you make today will have positive lasting impact.

EDUCATION AND CAREER PATHWAYS

INCOME   EXPENSES   DEBTS

INVESTMENTS   FUTURE   HAPPINESS

THE ACTIONS YOU TAKE EACH DAY MOULD YOU TO WHO YOU ARE TODAY.

WHO DO YOU WANT TO BE TOMORROW?

About the Authors

Dr Koh N.K. is the founder of FinTech Academy which spearheads talent development programmes and certifications for fintech in Singapore, and Advisor to the Institute of Blockchain, Singapore, which offers certification courses in blockchain. She is also the co-author of *Singapore: The Fintech Nation (2020)*.

Dr Koh was advisor to the NTU Investment Interactive Club (NTU-IIC) at the National Institute of Education, Nanyang Technological University, where she initiated financial literacy programmes and education activities for undergraduates and educators. She was also the chair of Citi-NIE Financial Literacy Hub for Teachers.

Chris Teo is the founder of SmartCo, an education company that imparts values to future-proof one's financial well-being through fun and engaging content. He has conceptualised various educational tech products throughout his career, advocating technology and gamification in learning.

He has designed learning workshops on financial literacy and universal positive values. Based on proven pedagogies and foundational learning theories, these have been well received by students and teachers in Singapore schools. The programmes are supported through grants by the Monetary Authority of Singapore, the Ministry of Education and other government agencies. He has also worked with financial institutions such as HSBC, Citibank and Maybank to deliver financial education to more than 50,000 students in Singapore since 2017.